T0364643

CRIMSON PAPERS

Reflections on Struggle, Suffering,
and Creativity in Pakistan

CRIMSON PAPERS

Reflections on Struggle, Suffering,
and Creativity in Pakistan

HARRIS KHALIQUE

OXFORD
UNIVERSITY PRESS

Oxford University Press is a department of the University of Oxford.
It furthers the University's objective of excellence in research, scholarship,
and education by publishing worldwide. Oxford is a registered trade mark of
Oxford University Press in the UK and in certain other countries

Published in Pakistan by
Ameena Saiyid, Oxford University Press
No.38, Sector 15, Korangi Industrial Area,
PO Box 8214, Karachi-74900, Pakistan

ISBN 978-0-19-940732-3

Typeset in Adobe Garamond Pro
Printed on 70gsm Woodfree Paper

Printed by VVP

In memoriam

Shayan Afzal Khan (Poppy)

Contents

Preface

MIRZA ASADULLAH KHAN GHALIB, THE GREAT BOHEMIAN POET and prominent nineteenth century Muslim counter-culturist, bore witness to the fall of the Mughal Empire. He says in Urdu:

Har Qadam Duuri-i-Manzil Haiy Numaayaan Mujh Se
Meri Raftaar Se Bhaagey Haiy Bayaabaan Mujh Se

Rendered into English, this reads:

With each step I take, the destination retreats
An expanding wilderness outpaces me

I have always felt that poetry is the only consistent thing in my otherwise tumultuous life. Poetry continues to capture people's imaginations even though we live in an age where fiction is written in haste and sold in abundance. Yet what I present here is neither poetry nor fiction but essays that offer an evaluation of social and political events through which individual and national histories are shaped. They provide a commentary on the evolution of society, polity, and the literary ethos of Pakistan in a broad South Asian context.

I write about those who were impacted by historic decisions they were not a part of. I write about wounds that have been festering across the South Asian subcontinent since 1947. I write about people who were dreamers and strove to make their dreams come true. I write about believers and non-believers who coexisted. I write about experiences and ideas that shaped my mind and that of so many others. I write about five women of the post-Independence generations who characterize the experience of living and dying in Pakistan. I write about people who paid in blood for the causes they espoused. I write about literature, mostly poetry, for that is my chief concern. Why must I write about all this? More hauntingly, what difference will it make if any at all?

It is crucial to write and reflect now for what could have once been considered an ordinary tale of a people has suddenly become important and needs to be told. I am conscious of both the isolation that has descended upon Pakistan in the imagination of other nations and the ripping existential stress Pakistan has been experiencing for the longest period of time. In this journey, I have seen how closely individuals shape the struggle and how politics shapes individuals.

In the realm of art—poetry, literature, film, theatre, painting, dance, and music—Pakistanis traditionally fought against censorship by the state and against curbs on freedom of expression imposed by military and civilian rulers. What we face now is a different kind of threat. There is a war waged against nuance, wit, complexity, subtlety, ambivalence, and the very possibility of creating art. We are in a conflict with absolutism, which has gained a life of its own. In that regard, it is immaterial in the most immediate sense whether religious absolutism was promoted in our region as a neo-colonial project at one point or whether it is now a by-product of Western imperial ambition.

At one end of the spectrum, we have thinkers like Terry Eagleton and Reza Aslan rationally explaining the rise of radicalism in Muslim societies that is seen to be targeting the Western world. At the other end are people like Richard Dawkins and Sam Harris who see a problem with the very conception of religious beliefs and practices. It is important for both sides to understand that it is not Western civilization which is under threat. It is Muslim civilization overall and, in our case, South Asian pluralism which is in danger of extinction. This conflict can only be resolved through the promotion of cultural pluralism, respect for diverse religious beliefs, and a demand for freedom of expression coupled with an unequivocal rejection of monocracy of any kind.

The suffering Pakistan bears today is caused by internal stress which is linked to its external tensions. Pakistanis, as people, are primarily conditioned by the partition of the South Asian subcontinent that resulted in the creation of their country in 1947 and subsequently by the dismemberment of Pakistan and the creation of Bangladesh in 1971. Today, Pakistan and India maintain a permanent discord with Kashmir remaining the principal signifier of this animosity. They have fought wars. The Line of Control and the Working Boundary drawn in 1948 in Kashmir are kept heated and the partition of the South Asian subcontinent remains an unresolved business.

Meanwhile, just as the line drawn by Radcliffe in 1947 defines Pakistan's eastern border with India, the line drawn by Durand in 1893 defines its western border with Afghanistan. Sir Mortimer Durand and Sir Cyril Radcliffe were British civil servants when they fulfilled their roles as glorified draftsmen who defined the country's geography and, in so doing, the country itself.

With Afghanistan, Pakistan has another unstable relationship at the moment defined by deep strains of mistrust running from top to bottom on both sides. We are told time and again by some Pakistani analysts and strategists that the complexity of the inter-state relationship between Pakistan and India is far more difficult to resolve than the differences that exist between Pakistan and Afghanistan. Pakistan has fought four wars with India. The two counties have supported anti-state movements in each other's territories and, instead of resolving longstanding disputes, have created new issues for each other along the way. This has not been the case with Afghanistan. Pakistan supported Afghans in getting the Soviet Union ousted from their country. About five million Afghan refugees lived in Pakistan for three decades and around three million remain even now. The Afghan economy is linked to the transit trade through Pakistan and thousands of Afghans travel to Pakistan on a daily basis—with or without visas.

These are some sound arguments. However, somehow I feel differently. After visiting Kabul and having met Afghan friends and colleagues in Islamabad on several occasions, it is evident that the relationship between Pakistan and Afghanistan is more unpleasant than the one Pakistan has with India. Pakistan and Afghanistan need an immediate and thorough revision in policy and practice.

On deep internal stresses within Pakistan, what needs to be remembered is that the idea of any country is as worthwhile as its citizens consider it to be. Being part of a state is about consensus while citizenship is about belonging. From the beginning, Pakistan had its own set of conflicts: between the native and the immigrant, the rich and the poor, the West Pakistani and the East Pakistani, the conservative and the liberal, and the soldier and the citizen. The conflict between the West Pakistani and the East Pakistani was resolved in blood to be replaced by a sharpening of the differences between the dwellers of the remaining provinces. The new contradiction to emerge in Pakistan's society and polity is between the worldview of the haughty, affluent, urban middle class and that of the rest of the citizenry.

David Grossman, Israeli author and a recognized voice for peace in the Middle East, made a speech after going through the tragedy of losing his son in the war waged by Israel against Palestine and Lebanon in 2006. Grossman said that he wrote about the life of his tortured country, which is drugged to the point of overdose by history, by emotions beyond what humans can contain, by an excess of events and tragedy, and by an exceeding amount of fear and a crippling sobriety.

I can relate to the pain of creative artists who find their own people wrong at times. Not just that, it is more unfortunate when they bear a personal loss for a collective cause that they may not have believed in. British fiction writer Julian Barnes' take on patriotism is worth quoting here. He says in one of his noted works of fiction, *Flaubert's Parrot*, 'the greatest patriotism is to tell your country when it is behaving dishonourably, foolishly, viciously.' If you choose that path, it gives you some moral strength to comment on other peoples and other countries without being prejudiced. In the four long essays here, I, too, make an attempt to write about the life of my tortured country from its beginning to the present day. I also tell the story of the ordinary people of South Asia whose suffering does not seem to end.

The first essay, titled 'Blood', begins by highlighting the issues of identity, communalism, and Kashmir leading up to independence from the British. It also talks about the dismemberment of British India and the subsequent creation of India and Pakistan in 1947 and Bangladesh in 1971. It analyses the perpetual conflicts resulting in occasional wars and then comes to what is happening currently in the region offering a critique of the dominant and competing narratives propounded by the ruling elites of these countries.

The second essay, titled 'Sweat', traces and chronicles the life, character, contribution, and struggle of some individuals belonging to the generation that was young at the time of Independence and the creation of Pakistan in 1947—those who believed in a progressive ideology. Some sung and some unsung, these people may not have succeeded in getting their ideals realized but left indelible marks on the minds of others and impacted political discourse. I had the privilege of knowing some of them through my father who was a part of the Progressive Movement.

The third essay, titled 'Tears', brings forth the experience of the post-Independence generations in Pakistan including my own. It is structured around five Pakistani women who, to me, characterize the country's present times. Three of them were assassinated, one languishes in prison, and one lost her young son and son-in-law in a bomb blast. There are other stories and experiences of life and death within these five narratives woven into an analysis of religious extremism, sectarianism, persecution of minorities, ethnic strife, provincial separatism, and shrinking of cultural and intellectual space.

The fourth and final essay in this collection, titled 'Ink', is about the creative response to Pakistan's political and social experience essentially through poetry. It begins with the issues of language and power in the country but then moves on to how I view the literary scene and the role and significance of poetry as a form of art. The essay highlights not just the corpus and strength of Urdu writing over the past few decades and how it reflects on what we went and are going through but also the richness offered by modern and contemporary Pakistani poetry. It is because of art and creativity in Pakistan that hope refuses to sink in the deluge of sorrow.

Harris Khalique
Islamabad, 2016

1

Blood

Hither I come to seek the spring
— John Donne

IN 1948, SUBSEQUENT TO THE CEASEFIRE BETWEEN INDIA AND Pakistan in the Kashmir Valley, the River Neelum is declared a part of the 'Line of Control' between the two countries. There is a dog from the village of Tetwal, on the banks of the Neelum, who has a habit of roaming about freely with no respect for the newly established territorial boundary. Initially, a few soldiers on both sides develop a liking for the dog. Out of affection, he is given an absurd name, *Chapar Jhun Jhun*, by Indian soldiers and an equally silly, *Sapar Sun Sun*, by Pakistanis. Eventually, the dog is shot dead on the suspicion of spying as his identity could not be established by the soldiers on either side. This famous Urdu short story, *Tetwal Ka Kutta*, was written by Saadat Hasan Manto and published in 1951.

When I add salt to my cup of boiling hot Kashmiri chai on a chilly Islamabad evening unlike my friends who prefer adding sugar, what comes to mind is not just this short story by Manto but also what my mother used to say when I was a boy. When fed up with my antics, she quoted an old quatrain in Persian about how characteristically low, mean, and miserly among the Asian races are Afghans, Kambohs, and Kashmiris—in that same pecking order. Except that even here, she would say wryly, Kashmiris could not claim the first spot.

Kashmir occupies a special place in the minds of most South Asians and its mention evokes a response, either political or cultural. The idea of the 'Vale of Cashmere' and the exquisite charm of its landscape and its dwellers enjoys a cardinal position in people's imagination. The reasons for that may vary from the references made in mythology and history to its spectacular natural splendour. Our children today can hardly figure out any phonetic differences between the languages spoken in their distant ancestral land and others in the larger region of both Pakistan and northern India. Because we are Pakistanis, we cannot visit Srinagar easily and introduce them to the splendours of the physical landscape of their familial past. The only person amongst my close friends in Pakistan who has been to Srinagar, the capital of the State of Jammu and Kashmir, is Tarique Rehman Fazlee.

Many years ago, in Fazlee's office in Urdu Bazaar, Karachi, some friends including Dr Shershah Syed, Mubin Mirza, Irfan Ahmad Khan, and Usman Qazi were discussing a new spate of tensions between India and Pakistan. Dr Syed and I had a heated argument on the issue—a usual happenstance in those years when I lived in Karachi. Syed sarcastically said that he was surprised to not see Pakistan's Foreign Office making me lead the peace talks with India. 'Kashmir is your land after all,' he added.

Inherited taste buds aside, Kashmir is more of an academic and intellectual interest than an emotional connection for most whose ancestors migrated from the Valley to other places in South Asia or beyond. These people have a much greater sense of belonging to places where they were born, educated, worked, and lived for generations—from Lucknow and Banaras to Sialkot and Lahore. There is certainly an association with their ancestral land that is felt among them particularly because the descendants of those who have been persecuted, for one reason or the other, are never made to forget that. Most of all, the inhabitants of Kashmir today continue to suffer and this conflict between India and Pakistan remains a perpetual cause for discontent in the whole region of South Asia.

****

We are a sentimental lot in Pakistan. We are angry. Either we hate or we worship. When it comes to India, Pakistanis are either in love with the idea of a secular India, believing it has already materialized while their own country rots and decomposes, or they consider everything Indian as an open or disguised plot for absolute Hindu ascendancy aimed at destroying the great Pakistani state and its people. It is ever more difficult to put an objective view across. For those who believe that India is as great as Jawaharlal Nehru's 'Tryst with Destiny', the fabulous Independence speech he made in 1947, Pakistan is undeniably always at fault. When it comes to India's Muslims or other minorities, these people either evade the questions by staying mute or they make inconsequential points by mentioning film stars, musicians, and dress designers of Muslim origin who are doing well in India. According to them, those Muslims from struggling classes who complain are backward like their kin in Pakistan or other parts of the Muslim world.

The anti-Indian feeling in Pakistan stems from a deep mistrust after fighting multiple wars. There are two types of people: those who harbour animosity towards India and those who also believe in that animosity's permanence. One group is those realist liberals who not only understand the role of the military in Pakistan, in the choices the country makes for itself but also peep through a narrow window of history and see India as essentially a Hindu state committed to suppressing Pakistan. They are convinced that no peace is possible between the countries in the foreseeable future. These people dismiss the arguments made by their counterpart Indian liberals. For instance, when A. P. J. Abdul Kalam is made the ceremonial head of state as a reward for masterminding the country's strategic defence programme, it is taken to be akin to Ottoman Turks using Armenian Generals to massacre Armenians, or Stalin as a Georgian consolidating the Russian empire in the name of the Soviet Union; or Marshal Tito, himself a Croat, letting the Serbians become more powerful than any other people in the then Yugoslavia including his own Croats.

The other quintessentially anti-Indian group comprises of Islamic fundamentalists whose ideology is a mutation of faith germinated in the Pakistani seminaries and think tanks, which enjoy the patronage of the very same religious parties and schools of thought that stood against the creation of Pakistan in the first place. Yet now, for them, Islam and Pakistan are mutually interchangeable concepts with the same meaning. They continue to whip up emotions against India.

The anti-Indian sentiments in Pakistan are further fuelled by the new rise in India of the Rashtriya Swayamsevak Sangh (RSS), its powerful protégé and successor, the Bharatiya Janata Party (BJP), and the increasingly dismal state of minority rights in India, whether we speak of Muslims, Sikhs, or Christians. From Amritsar in Punjab to Bhubaneswar in Orissa, religious minorities are not just at risk but have borne the wrath of the majority.

India's military overtures towards Israel in the recent past have further agitated the Pakistani mind. Without getting into the debate about India mending fences with powers that it considered imperial and exploitative in the past, what is immediate for the conservative Pakistani mind is the idea of the Hindu and the Jew coming together to annihilate Pakistan. Most Pakistanis have little or no knowledge about Egypt, Turkey, and Jordan having full diplomatic ties with Israel for a number of decades. They also do not know about Operation Black September in 1967 when General Zia ul-Haq, then a Brigadier on secondment from the Pakistan Army, led the massacre of Palestinians at the behest of the Jordanian king.

India working with Israel is therefore considered a unique threat by Pakistan. Perhaps it is. But Pakistanis need to look around and see that the United Arab Emirates and Saudi Arabia are least bothered about what India has to do with Israel and the conflict between India and Pakistan. They continue to foster a strong economic and strategic relationship with India. In early 2016, Saudi Arabia conferred its highest civil award on the Indian prime minister. Afghanistan and

Iran, the two Muslim neighbours of Pakistan, have also developed close commercial and economic ties with India. The Islamic world that Pakistan takes pride in being a part of is increasingly indifferent to Pakistan's position on its unresolved issues with India.

****

On the other side of the border, in India, R. K. Narayan, the master storyteller, begins his essay, *The Problem of the Indian Writer*, which I read sometime in 1999, by stating that all imaginative writing in India has had its origin in the Ramayana and the Mahabharata, the 10,000-year-old epics. Elaborating his point, he says that these traditions were modified by historical changes and asks his readers to skip a great deal of intervening history and come down to British times. One wouldn't have expected R. K. Narayan, a man of incredible literary genius, to show a disrespect for history comparable to that shown on the other side of the border by some historians.

Undoubtedly, there are some historians and social commentators in Pakistan today who think that the history of the subcontinent began in 712 AD when Mohammed bin Qasim invaded Sindh, and then the next chapter began in 1947. But, they do not enjoy the standing in the world of letters that Narayan does. The problem is that what Narayan refers to as 'intervening history', produced not scores but hundreds of cultural icons, musicians, artistic and literary geniuses in India from Tan Sen and Amir Khusro to Mir Taqi Mir and Vali Deccani. And above all, Mirza Ghalib, a household name across South Asia.

During and after British times, from Allama Mohammed Iqbal to Saadat Hasan Manto, Brij Narain Chakbast, Rajinder Singh Bedi, Krishan Chander, Ismat Chughtai, Qurratul Ain Hyder, Josh Malihabadi, Firaq Gorakhpuri (whose real name was Raghopati Sahai), Noon Meem Rashid, and Faiz Ahmed Faiz, all of these writers are rooted in that 'intervening history'. Manipulation of a great deal of intervening history on the one hand combined with the insistence on that history being the only period of magnificence on the other, led to the communal partition of British India.

From the occasional, but always lethal, Hindu-Muslim riots in the past, to the seething intolerance that has enveloped all communities living across South Asia recently, to events like the demolition of the Babri Mosque in 1992 and the Gujarat pogroms in 2002, each simply adds new, more complicated turns to the spiral of communal and inter-state relations in the subcontinent. The raid on the Golden Temple in Amritsar, the murder of Indira Gandhi by her own guards who were Sikh, and the ensuing anti-Sikh riots in 1984 further proved that the idea of a secular India is yet to be realized.

Many years ago, I had a strikingly similar experience, on two different occasions, with two highly educated and thoroughly refined Indian Muslims. Writer Mahmood Hashmi in Delhi, and writer and broadcaster Yawar Abbas in London, virtually asked me to withdraw all the militants Pakistan had sent across the border to support the insurgency in Kashmir. Abbas, undoubtedly, was more subtle and sophisticated. But it felt for a moment, on both occasions, that the gentlemen thought that I was the one who commanded the army in Kargil, or worked directly under the command of, say Lt General Hameed Gul, to mobilize infiltration in Kashmir.

However, putting anger into context can make you sympathize with the one who is angry. In today's India—not always, but on a number of occasions—I have seen secular Muslims going through a test of fire to prove their unequivocal allegiance to the country. They made me go through the same *agnipariksha* (akin to the test of fire Lord Ram had put his beloved wife Sita through) to prove that I condemned any extremism and militancy. R. K. Narayan is not entirely wrong after all.

There are the Pankaj Misras, Pavan Varmas, and Mukul Kesawans in India who take a much wider view of the Indian ethos, including, as they do, the Indo-Persian civilization and the Indo-Muslim culture. But the mainstream narrative in India is increasingly held hostage to the politics of exclusion and the construction of a typical Indian—a 'Vijay Kumar'—like there is a typical Pakistani, a 'Javed Iqbal'.

****

In 2014, Indians elected Narendra Modi as their prime minister. A democrat anywhere, however reluctantly, will respect the mandate given to him by the people of India. But in order to make us forget the views held by him and his compatriots about Muslims and other minorities in India, such as Christians—and, of course, the belligerence shown towards Pakistan by him and his close aides in the recent past, he has more ground to cover than any other politician.

Another interesting twist is Mr Modi's departure from being a karsewak (a committed volunteer activist in the Hindu revivalist movement) and from his mother institution, the RSS, in terms of being pro-liberalization, encouraging a market economy, and supporting globalization. It is interesting to witness the economic agenda of the Hindu right changing as many in the Indian middle and lower-middle classes get jobs in the short run as a result of those policies, but their religious agenda becomes more steadfast.

Modi is still seen as complicit in the horrendous anti-Muslim riots in Gujarat in 2002. His party is responsible for razing the Babri Mosque in Ayodhya, UP. It is not just about the Hindutva rhetoric; he, and those he is surrounded by, successfully made possible the translation of that rhetoric into bloodletting and wide-scale unrest. No one expects him to change the fundamental character of his party, his own views, or the inclinations of his constituency overnight. Hailing from a right-wing religious and political platform, the person holding the highest executive office is now expected to negotiate between two competing views of the world in India: one is that of Zakia Jafri and the other that of Maya Kodnani.

Zakia Jafri is the wife of Ehsan Jafri, a veteran politician who remained a parliamentarian from Ahmedabad as a leader of Congress. He was hacked and burnt to death, in his home, by a mob during the infamous Gulbarg Society incident amid the Gujarat riots. He was 72 years-old then, also a poet with an acclaimed collection of Urdu verse *Qandeel* to his name. Zakia had been fighting the case against the perpetrators that named Narendra Modi as a suspect. After going through layers and layers of investigative and judicial processes, the metropolitan court dismissed the case in December 2013. Zakia was determined to fight it further.

Maya Kodnani, whose parents migrated from Tharparkar, Sindh, and settled in the state of Gujarat at the time of Partition, was a BJP legislator from Naroda. She and her husband are medical doctors by profession. It is ironic that she was the minister of women and children welfare at the time of the Gujarat pogrom of 2002. Ironic and painful because women and children suffer the most during, and in the aftermath of, every conflict—the more violent the conflict, the more suffering it brings to survivors. Kodnani was convicted and sentenced to twenty-eight years in prison after evidence was found that she organized the massacre of ninety-five people in her constituency. Prime Minister Narendra Modi, or any conservative religious government that comes to power in India, has to keep reminding themselves that their choices, decisions, successes, and failings will directly impact every sixth human being in the world. And every third such human being will be a non-Hindu. Therefore any communally-driven or anti-minority policy, or action taken in India will further drag the whole region into an unending cycle of hatred and violence.

In 2015, Prime Minister Modi visited Bangladesh. He was presented a large framed photograph by Sheikh Hasina Wajid, the Prime Minister of Bangladesh and daughter of Sheikh Mujibur Rahman, the founder of Bangladesh. In this famous picture taken on 16 December 1971, Lt General A. A. K. Niazi of the Pakistan

Army is signing the instrument of surrender as Lt General Jagjit Singh Aurora of the Indian army looks on. This gesture by the Bangladeshi prime minister did not sit well with many Pakistanis, some of whom reiterated that Pakistan was not at fault in its eastern wing as India helped create Bangladesh.

Some of us believe that 1971 was a continuity of 1947. Jinnah, Pakistan's founding father, called what he got a 'truncated, moth-eaten Pakistan' showing his displeasure over the Radcliffe Boundary Commission Award that determined the borders of Pakistan in both the eastern and north-western parts of India. But he did not mention the absurdity of the new state's geography, where the two wings were separated by 1,500 miles of Indian territory in the middle. However, the reason Pakistan got dismembered was not simply absurd geography. Many today tend to forget that the British had divided Bengal along religious lines in 1905 for six years, and in the movement for the creation of Pakistan, the province had led from the front. Perhaps a loosely structured union between the two wings was possible, just as avoiding the Partition of India was possible had the Cabinet Mission Plan been accepted by the leadership of the Indian National Congress in 1946.

****

But just as 1947 cannot be reversed, what happened in 1971 cannot be overturned. I was in kindergarten when Pakistan was dismembered. I am told that a couple of years earlier, carrying me as an infant, my parents had visited East Pakistan. In Khulna, we stayed at the home of my father's uncle, Shoaib Warsi, nick-named Shubboo, who was the same age as my father and a dear friend. He was married to a cultured and refined lady from Kolkata who spoke both Bangla and Urdu. Warsi ran a transportation business and edited and published a newspaper in English. Shubboo Dada, which is what I used to call him when he had moved to Karachi after 1971, had to leave all his property behind in Bangladesh and virtually run for his life with his wife and three sons. He started from scratch and launched himself again in Karachi. His knack for profitable businesses was unmatched in the entire family. Shubboo Dada had patrician features, fair skin, silky silver-grey hair, and a typically hooked nose. He was never angry and had a great sense of humour. Dada had a serious side to him as well. He was grounded in classical Persian and Urdu poetry with considerable knowledge of Sanskrit, Bangla, and English literatures.

He was famous not only for openly swearing at friends and cousins in public to show his affection, but also for creating unique and destructive swear words. He would laugh out loud after cracking jokes and telling funny stories. Dada must have been quite a character in his youth. He told me that his father, who would always keep his cool, was once so irritated that he slapped him in public. The family elders were having tea after dinner and discussing the scarcity of opportunities for Muslim women to obtain a college education in Lucknow when Shubboo Dada decided to butt in. He suggested to his uncle, the elder brother of his father, that not only should the family now establish a girls' college for his own cousins and other Muslim girls to promote education among them, they should also name it the 'Kaul Girls College'. He said that this may also ensure employment for some after graduation. Kaul was our family's caste before they had converted to Islam in Kashmir. The word 'Kaul' is pronounced in the same way 'call' is pronounced in English.

My mother recalls that when we were being taken to Khulna Club one evening in 1969, by Shubboo Dada, in what was then East Pakistan, the car was attacked by a group of Bengali youth in the middle of the main bazaar, yelling and swearing at us, *Sala Bihari; Sala Panzabi; Maro! Maro! Sala Harami; Maro! Maro!* (Hit the bastards; they are Bihari; they are Punjabi), somehow figuring out that we were not Bengalis. Biharis were non-Bengali migrant Muslims from India who came after 1947 and now supported West Pakistan. Punjabis were considered oppressors of Bengal, and Biharis were their allies. Shubboo Dada and his driver tried to engage with the youth and pacify them, but since they were easily recognizable by their looks and demeanour, the mob refused to calm down. Eventually, the driver of the car rushed us out of the situation by means of his expert driving skills.

My father once narrated another incident from the same trip, or maybe another trip made around the same period to East Pakistan. Baby Islam, whose real name is Anwarul Islam, a leading cameraperson then, and who later came to be considered one of the pioneers of the Bangladeshi film industry, hosted a dinner in honour of my father and invited people associated with the arts, literature, music, and film to meet him. After dinner, people sat around the room sipping tea, when my father overheard one of the guests telling another that *Urdu kokorer bhasha aachay* (Urdu is the language of dogs). Urdu was one of the identity markers of the Muslims of British India and became the first state language of Pakistan before Bangla was made the second in 1952, subsequent to a Bangla language rights movement. Urdu was viewed as the language imposed by West Pakistan on East Pakistan. The person who made that remark about Urdu had no idea that my father knew Bangla well. The one he was speaking to knew though. He looked at my father and immediately understood that he had heard what was being said. He whispered something in the ear of the person who had said that. The man stood up, came straight to my father, and touched his feet. He apologized profusely and said that he would never want to hurt a guest, but a man like my father would understand what East Pakistan had gone through at the hands of the West Pakistani army, bureaucracy, businessmen, and political elite since 1947. He said it was sheer anger and pain that made him say that. Else, how could he ever think of demeaning the language of Ghalib and Iqbal?

My father first felt a little nervous and scared, and then alienated and numb. But he swiftly picked the man up from the floor and embraced him. At that point his host, Baby Islam, came forward and praised my father for being forgiving. He then said that he knew my father must have been hurt even if he did not say so. He was a guest from West Pakistan whom they cherished. He also regretted what had happened, but then told my father that he should think about how there were so few in West Pakistan who would bother to understand why things have come to this stage.

I am not sure whether it was first the suppression and then the assertion of identity markers like language that brought about the creation of Bangladesh. Jinnah's famous or infamous speech made in 1948 in Dhaka is seen by both independent and pro-Awami League commentators as sowing the seed of permanent discord between East and West Pakistan. There was an over-emphasis in his speech on Urdu as the only state language of Pakistan, and on the fact that every state needs a lingua franca. But in the same speech, he categorically mentioned that each province, including East Bengal, had the right to choose a language to conduct its business. There was no mention of a single 'national' language in his speech, or replacing other languages with Urdu in their respective habitats. However, both sides—the West Pakistanis and the East Pakistanis—used the Dhaka speech selectively to further their political agendas. Urdu was promoted as the only national language by the north Indian immigrant elite and their counterparts in Punjab to impose a unity on people, while they themselves continued to use English as the language of power.

It was after a language rights movement was initially crushed by the central government in Pakistan that Bangla was eventually declared Pakistan's second state and national language as early as 1952. Nonetheless, Bengalis chose not to stay with the rest of Pakistan as the shabby treatment meted out to them did not end with Bangla becoming one of the two officially recognized national languages. It is therefore not just about language; it is about not getting a fair share in key jobs and economic resources, denial of social justice, and not being awarded political rights with dignity that makes people seek freedom. When there was martial rule and a large part

of the military came from a limited number of districts in two out
of five provinces, alienation increased exponentially. Language only
served as a rallying point for the people who wanted their rights
to be realized.

****

When a seasoned journalist and leading columnist of the Urdu
language, Wusatullah Khan, started translating sections of General
Ayub Khan's diaries from English into Urdu for the BBC Urdu news
website my interest was reignited in what happened during the last
years of a united Pakistan. This led me to read new accounts and re-
read some old ones. There is a famous description of Bengalis that
General Ayub Khan gives in his book, *Friends Not Masters*, which says
that the people of Pakistan consist of a variety of races, each with its
own historical background and culture, and East Bengalis probably
belong to the original Indian races. It would be no exaggeration he
continues to say that up to the creation of Pakistan they had not
known any real freedom or sovereignty. They have been ruled in turn
either by caste Hindus, Mughals, Pathans, or the British. He goes
on with his rant and says that they have been, and still are, under
Hindu cultural and linguistic influence. As such, they have all the
inhibitions of downtrodden races and have not yet found it possible
to psychologically adjust to the requirements of a new-born freedom.
He says that their complexes—exclusiveness, suspicion, and a sort
of defensive aggressiveness—probably emerge from this historical
background. Now this is the self-proclaimed five-star General, the
Field Marshal, the President of Pakistan, and the first Martial Law
Administrator, Mohammad Ayub Khan, judging in his political
autobiography the majority of his own countrymen and women back
in the 1960s. What else do you call racism? What else do you call
ignorance? What did Ayub mean by real freedom or sovereignty and
East Pakistanis being ruled forever by high caste Hindus, Mughals,
Pathans, and the British? Where else in the subcontinent were peasants

and workers ruling their states or regions? Was there democracy in Ayub's native village where he was born in 1907 and probably rode on the back of a mule to go to school? What does he mean by Hindu cultural and linguistic influence? It is shocking that people with such a limited understanding of human society and a warped sense of history have ruled Pakistan with impunity.

As far as culture is concerned, Pakistanis are South Asians first, with influences from West and Central Asia. The faith that is practised and rituals that are observed add further distinctiveness within the regional and local cultural traditions. Most North Indian languages, including Ayub's mother tongue Hindko, are derived from Sanskrit and Prakrits. Ironic! Hindko is the only language spoken in today's Pakistan which has the word 'Hind' in its name. Ayub was oblivious to the Bengalis' contribution to knowledge and civilization in the Indian subcontinent, including the Muslim culture of this region. His observations about East Bengalis came at a time when the great Bangla poet Kazi Nazrul Islam was alive and revered across all of East Pakistan. Ayub talks about the inhibitions of the downtrodden Bengalis which made it hard for them to understand what it meant to be liberated. He listed those inhibitions as popular complexes, exclusiveness, suspicion, and a sort of defensive aggression. He was speaking about East Pakistanis, but unfortunately Ayub's own superior 'West Pakistanis' seem to suffer from these inhibitions. He sounds so right in defining a people. But the people he is describing are his own: those who live in Pakistan today. The popular myth, however, endures that Bangladesh became a country only because of its forfeited right to use its language. It is not only in politics that perception is more important than reality, but to appropriate from Maulana Abul Kalam Azad's seminal work on Sufi Sarmad Shaheed, a myth cannot be challenged once the majority begins to accept it as the eternal truth.

More than twenty-five years after my father's last visit to East Pakistan, I visited Bangladesh for a few weeks in 1995. I could see in the eyes of my otherwise hospitable hosts that they saw me under the halo of West Pakistan, the Pakistan Army, and Urdu. My friend Zafar Junejo and I had brought a gift from our common friend, Javed Bhutto for a Bangla writer Panna Kaiser, who was based in Dhaka. She invited us to her place for breakfast. A tall, fair, middle-aged woman, clad in an elegant sari warmly welcomed us. After we settled down and had an initial exchange of pleasantries, she told us that we were the first Pakistanis to visit her house since the liberation of Bangladesh. It was a big deal. Some of her and her late husband's friends were unhappy when she mentioned that two young Pakistani men are visiting her. But her daughter, Shomi Kaiser, a young woman who was already a famous actor convinced her mother to go ahead with her plans to invite us and said it is time to move on and bury the hatchet. Besides, the two guests who were arriving had nothing to do with 1971. When I got to know that she was also the widow of the famous journalist and writer, Shaheedullah Kaiser, I told her about her husband's association with my father. An association based on their shared interests and literary pursuits.

Shaheedullah Kaiser was among those journalists, writers, academics, and intellectuals who were allegedly picked up by the activists of pro-West Pakistan militias and killed. I call these militias—mainly the Razakars, Al-Badr, and Al-Shams—pro-West Pakistan and not pro-Pakistan. East Pakistan was as much Pakistan as West Pakistan when that grave tragedy began to unfold. East Pakistan did not just have a larger population than West Pakistan, but it also had sacrificed and struggled more than those in the western wing for a separate homeland for South Asian Muslims.

Unfortunately, the dominant West Pakistani elite and state institutions never got it right; social oppression, economic exploitation, undignified behaviour, and political marginalization continued until the end. Measures taken to appease the citizens after the general elections in 1970 were mere eyewash. In the psyche of a West Pakistani barring those who supported the National Awami Party (NAP) in those years, Bengalis were traitors. The process of separation has blood smeared all over its face. Bangladesh finally came into being after the mandate of the winning party (Awami League) was thoroughly violated in the general elections in Pakistan in 1970. Political space was not provided to resolve outstanding issues between the two wings of the country. A brutal military operation was undertaken instead and India decided to intervene militarily.

Mujibur Rahman, the leader of the Awami League who later became the founder of Bangladesh, had emerged as the popular leader nationally, but not the main leader of West Pakistan. It was Zulfikar Ali Bhutto and his Pakistan People's Party (PPP) who achieved astounding success in the 1970 general elections across the Punjab and Sindh provinces in the West. Therefore, Zulfikar Ali Bhutto and the PPP of that era have to share considerable blame for the debacle. When one political party allows force to be used against its civilian political adversaries a vicious cycle begins. Bhutto himself was hanged eight years later by the same army whose actions against the Awami League he had supported.

How ironic that the majority of Pakistanis chose to secede from the country they had created. Much has been written, debated, and argued on the subject. But there has not been fair closure in either Bangladesh or Pakistan. It was important for Bangladesh to investigate the military high-handedness committed during 1971 as well as the violence and bloodletting in the streets, public places, and homes across many cities and villages that caused hundreds of thousands of deaths and other casualties, and to bring to book those who were responsible for inflicting pain and suffering on its citizens. Those who aided or abetted the army in carrying out its operations, or those who participated in silencing any voices of dissent against the West Pakistan-dominated state narrative at the time are seen as criminals in Bangladesh. For Generals like Yahya Khan, Tikka Khan, Farman Ali, and A. A. K. Niazi, East Pakistanis fighting them were traitors. For the then East Pakistanis and now Bangladeshis, those siding with these Generals are traitors. After more than four decades having passed many Pakistanis today agree that the Awami League should have been allowed to form the government in Islamabad after the results of the 1970 elections.

****

In Dhaka it took them a long time to start the process of investigating war crimes committed in 1971. That is still better than not having a process of fixing responsibility at all. However, for the sake of sanity and well-being in their own society the process should have been more about establishing the truth; apportioning responsibility on individuals, groups, outfits, and institutions where needed; sanctioning and constraining those found responsible; asking the guilty to offer an unconditional apology to their nation and seek forgiveness from the families and friends of victims; and the proceedings of any trials should have been fully impartial and transparent.

The death penalty is the maximum punishment that is awarded and is of course completely irrevocable. For those involved in heinous crimes, banning their outfits and putting their members behind bars for the rest of their lives may have sufficed. Also, for the sake of humanity and to keep the record straight and transparent, acts of militias like the Mukti Bahini against civilians should also have been investigated and recorded. Fighting with the military, attacking combatant soldiers or their active abetters may well be justified with time as history progresses, but the killings of civilians by liberation forces and militias cannot be rationalized in the name of excesses committed during any war. It is detrimental to the emotional and intellectual development of any society if it decides to look the other way, or become selective with facts, when it comes to atrocities committed by those militants whose cause is considered just by that society.

In Pakistan, one resolution adopted by the National Assembly and then the statements made by some leading politicians condemned

the hanging of the Jamaat-i-Islami leaders in Bangladesh, Abdul
Quader Molla and Motiur Rahman Nizami. They were involved in
the killings of Awami League workers, academics and intellectuals, and
innocent East Pakistanis. The resolution and these statements issued
in Pakistan hint at an equally disturbing and deep-seated problem in
the Pakistani psyche which is comparable to what was happening to
the Bangladeshi mind at that time. Pakistan recognizes Bangladesh
as an independent, sovereign country since 1974. These hangings
are entirely an internal matter of that country and some Pakistani
parliamentarians have trespassed into a domain that is not theirs.
Who are they to ask Bangladesh to open or not to open cases against
people who were involved in violence against Bangladeshi citizens-
to-be in 1971?

Pakistanis are troubled and feel confused when it comes to setting
the record straight, bringing resolution and closure to issues that
have plagued our social and political consciousness, and accepting
collectively what went wrong without being defensive. In this case,
we could never put out the full text of the Hamoodur Rehman
Commission report, never even attempted to try those who are
responsible for what we see as a debacle and a national tragedy. We
have neither found nor established fair responsibility on any occasion,
having kept all investigations out of bounds for the public at large, and
never even charging any of the assassins of our leaders from Liaquat Ali
Khan to Benazir Bhutto. And now, Pakistani politicians had the gall
to ask Bangladeshis to sweep their history under the carpet like we are
used to doing with ours. I am not sure if the young parliamentarians in
Pakistan even remember the fate of more than two 250,000 Pakistanis
stranded in the refugee camps set up by the UN in Bangladesh after
its liberation. These were the civilians whose forbearers had migrated
from the provinces of Bihar and UP in India to East Pakistan after
Partition in 1947. They were loyal to a united Pakistan until the last
moment. Their next generations are still in the camps of Mirpur and
Mohammadpur on the outskirts of Dhaka.

Before, during, and after the war in 1971, many non-Bengali Pakistanis settled in East Pakistan were able to migrate to West Pakistan traversing sea, land, or air routes via Kolkata, Kathmandu, and Colombo. Their arrival in Karachi marked the second wave of migration to West Pakistan, which soon became just Pakistan after the liberation of Bangladesh. The migration of Muslims to Pakistan from those parts of India where they were in a minority was a unique phenomenon and impacted the politics and sociology of the country unlike any other state. Let me comment on the issue in another essay.

****

The Partition of India and creation of Pakistan that came along with the Independence of the subcontinent from British colonialism, and the subsequent dismemberment of Pakistan and liberation of Bangladesh, not only remain an unresolved business, the gaps that were created have widened with time. The subconscious narrative of the state of Pakistan continues to define the country as 'non-India'. The gate at the Wagah border near Lahore, providing official entry into and exit from the two countries' territory, is called *Bab-i-Azadi* (The Gate to Freedom), by Pakistan. We were not freed from India; we were freed from the British. The Indian state, on the other hand, browbeats its smaller neighbours and in the same spirit wants a compliant neighbour on its western border.

The two countries kill the villagers who live along the Line of Control and the Working Boundary in Kashmir, catch and imprison poor fisher folk who unknowingly trespass the lines drawn on water, support secessionist movements through proxy outfits and under cover agents within each other's borders, and spend colossal amounts of money on the arms race. The privileged Indian and Pakistani old boys drink together to the nostalgia of Doon School, Dehradun; Government College, Lahore; St. Stephen's College, Delhi; as well as Sandhurst, Oxford, and Cambridge, and get their children to establish contact with each other in foreign lands. But it is more of a cultivated social relationship between the same class of people, who at the same time may be benefiting from the economy of tension, insecurity, jingoism, and war. Their contacts are seldom seriously intended to bring the two countries together. The poor languish in each other's jails, while the rich Cambridge alumni from India and Pakistan remember college days they spent together and raise toasts in the Avari Hotel, Lahore, and Le Meridien Hotel, New Delhi. Lt General A. A. K. Niazi dies in his comfortable bed in Pakistan at a ripe old age while Sepoy Maqbool Hussain spends forty years of his youth and senior years in an Indian prison with his tongue slashed.

For some strange reason, the life and suffering of Sepoy Maqbool Hussain brings to my mind the life and suffering of Amena Iffat, although the two lives seem to have nothing in common. Iffat was my mother's maternal aunt who had adopted and raised her. She occasionally composed poems and wrote fiction, led a dynamic social life, and joined the All-India Muslim League sometime in the 1940s. She had built a park, and established a school and vocational training centre for women in the city of Muzaffarnagar where she moved after her marriage. Amena Iffat was probably the first ever Muslim woman mayor of a city in British India. But after Independence in 1947, she could barely ever make ends meet. The unsettled lifestyle, the limited means, continued hardship, and the unending misery eventually started impacting her mental health. In 1972, after the death of her husband she lost her sanity. Whenever she felt a little better in the morning, she picked up the daily *Dawn* and told everyone gleefully that she likes reading this newspaper because it was founded by Quaid-i-Azam Mohammad Ali Jinnah. After her physical and mental health had completely broken down she was admitted to a mental asylum where she died in 1974.

After the creation of Pakistan, Jinnah had said he intended to retire to Mumbai. Gandhi expressed his wish to settle in Pakistan to bring the people of the two countries closer. The premise of Partition for them was to establish long lasting peace in the subcontinent. As a myth cannot be challenged once the majority begins to believe in it as the ultimate truth, Kashmir has become central to peace in South Asia whether that is a reality or not.

Besides the post-Partition issues around water resources and control over land by both India and Pakistan, I find it important to consult Prem Nath Bazaz's seminal work of the past, *The History of Struggle for Freedom in Kashmir*, to understand the context and causes for the long-lasting struggle. Also, the seeds that turned the Kashmiri nationalist movement into a Hindu-Muslim issue were there from the past, but the communal division was further highlighted once Pakistan started playing a role in emboldening the dividing lines. Kashmiri Pandits, historically the oldest sons and daughters of the Valley, had to leave in large numbers after they were attacked by Kashmiri Muslims. Today, fear and violence are the warp and weft of life in Kashmir. With the presence of a massive Indian military contingent and its excesses, I am reminded of the *azan* outside the Central Jail in Srinagar on 13 July 1931, punctuated by twenty-one young men in a row being shot one after the other by the police of the Maharaja of Jammu & Kashmir.

The periodic military interventions by Pakistan have not helped in resolving the issue either. I am one of those who subscribe to the idea that battles can be won and lost, but no one wins or loses a war. However, it is fair to accept that Pakistan could never overpower India. The reasons are many, first and foremost being the adage in English that God is always on the side of the bigger battalion. In 1948, the tribal warriors who were sent to Kashmir, with support from a nascent military, failed to penetrate the valley. The moment the Indian army arrived in Kashmir and retaliated, the march into Kashmir was brought to a halt. What Pakistan has under its control is the fringe of the State of Jammu & Kashmir and the areas of Gilgit-Baltistan. Ethnic Kashmiris from the valley do not consider these parts of the region as Kashmir proper. Even my aunt, who spoke

Urdu in a Lukhnavi accent and had little to do with Kashmiri politics
or culture besides dabbling in Kashmiri cuisine called *Wazwan* once
in a while, politely objected to the claim to Kashmiri identity made
by her Hindko-speaking domestic help from Muzaffarabad.

In 1965, when Operation Gibraltar, an incursion into Kashmir
was thoroughly unsuccessful and India invaded Pakistan, the best that
Pakistanis could do was defend the mainland for some days before
a ceasefire document was signed in Tashkent. The war was over in
seventeen days. Pakistan defended Lahore and successfully fought
the tank battle in Chawinda while its air force demonstrated initial
superiority. But any intended gains were made neither in Kashmir
nor elsewhere.

Air Marshal (retd.) Nur Khan, a highly respected air force
commander and soldier, reminiscing on the occasion of the fortieth
anniversary of the war in 2005, held that the performance of the
Pakistan Army did not match that of the Pakistan Air Force mainly
because the leadership was not as professional. They had planned
Operation Gibraltar for self-glory rather than the national interest. It
was a wrong war and people were misled into believing that the war
began with Indian aggression on Lahore. But Air Marshal Nur Khan,
a man who is virtually canonized by soldiers and civilians alike, and
who is held in high esteem across the board for his services in building
several national institutions, cannot be quoted that easily in public
for his views on the 1965 war.

On the fiftieth anniversary of the war, in 2015, when I took a view
slightly different from the norm within a closed group of my old
Pakistani classmates on social media, mostly engineers but including
a few serving in the military, all of them now in their middle age, I
was told that I had succumbed to Indian propaganda. If they stopped
short of calling me a traitor, it was only out of affection.

What happened in 1971, after Pakistan's military action in its
eastern wing against the most popularly elected political party, the
Awami League, and its supporters, and the subsequent intervention

by the Indian army, is another gruesome chapter in the blood-soaked political history of South Asia. Between India and Pakistan, the Kargil war was the last misadventure where men in uniform were directly involved. This happened even after both countries had detonated nuclear devices in 1998. India carried out its first nuclear tests in 1974 but when it went for another round in 1998, Pakistan followed suit. Since Kargil, there are proxies in the shape of militant outfits and secret agents who fight on behalf of the two nuclear armed neighbours. There have been other incidents, but the Mumbai attacks of 2008, where innocent civilians were killed in public places, left a deep scar on the already tarnished face of the relationship between the two countries. The regulars are only involved in keeping the guns and canons warm at the Line of Control and the Working Boundary in Kashmir. Or they maintain their belligerent positions on the cold and barren Siachen Glacier, which happens to house the highest military posts in the world, proudly established by two of the poorest of countries.

****

But who is wise in South Asia? The ardent peaceniks, the bleeding-heart liberals, the hopeful poets like this scribe? The sanguine historians and a segment of religious scholars tilted towards mysticism belonging to the subcontinent tell us with such fervour that ours is a land of sages and saints, women and men who believed in eternal peace and spiritual liberation. Men and women of God, His messengers, and the yogis and the sufis—from Gautam Buddha and Mahavira to Khwaja Moinuddin Chishti and Hazrat Nizamuddin Auliya, and from Guru Nanak to Swami Vivekanand—define us as people. We are told that the lives and teachings of these people are a source of inspiration for the rich and the poor alike, the ignorant and the knowledgeable, and for the majority and minority communities following any faith or sect. All that has happened contrary to the real nature of South Asia— battles, riots, loot, and plunder—was either an aberration, or the conspiracy of an outside force, an invading army, or a colonial power. There is a sense of pride, hidden or obvious, in being South Asian.

But is that really the case? Can we take pride in belonging to a region and civilization that harbours peace and tolerance? Can we claim to have accepted any kind of difference found within or outside with magnanimity? Do we really believe in the basic humanistic tenet of 'live and let live'? There may have been certain interludes in South Asian history when peace or relative peace prevailed in all or some parts of the region. But what is happening today within South Asian societies and among South Asian countries contradicts what the claimants of a superior, peaceful, divine, and spiritual South Asia profess.

Barring ghettos within the elite circles of South Asian metropolises, there is no tolerance, let alone acceptance, for any differences across the societies in which we live in India, Pakistan, and Bangladesh. It seems that people get tired of maligning, hurting, looting, and killing each other after some years. After catching their breath, they once again resort to the same methods of perpetrating violence and imposing their will over the other by coercion. After what happened in 1947, when millions had to forcibly migrate, hundreds of thousands were killed, and scores of young girls and women were kidnapped and raped, did West Pakistanis not repeat the same in 1971 and unleash terror on our own countrymen and women in East Pakistan? Muslims who lived in India for hundreds of years and chose to stay in their homeland at the time of the Partition of British India—most of them locals who had converted to Islam at some point in history anyway—are still seen as fifth columnists by many Hindus.

At the same time, in Pakistan—a country created on the basis of Muslim nationalism in the subcontinent—we saw ethnic and provincial divides surfacing and taking a violent turn from day one. In the larger Pakistani society, is there any tolerance whatsoever for people who think differently or even look different, let alone those who have a separate set of beliefs, speak a different language (or even a dialect), and come from a region in the country that is different from one's own? In a country founded on the basis of demands for maximum provincial autonomy and equal rights for those belonging to minority faiths—at least if you go by the vision of the founding father—smaller provinces and marginalized communities within the provinces continue to struggle for their due share in opportunities and resources to this day, while religious minorities are increasingly demeaned and deprived. The state's use of force to curb political movements in provinces and administrative regions other than Punjab happens to this day. Both non-Muslim and Muslim women and men are charged with blasphemy while Shia Muslims are targeted and killed in the length and breadth of the country. Proving right the prophetic academic of yesteryear, Wilfred Cantwell Smith, the Pakistani state has become to a large extent a confused theocracy. Pakistan's society is becoming more and more inward looking and the average Pakistani individual is becoming more and more conservative—culturally and politically. There is a kind of legitimacy among a part of the population with regard to oppression and violence against the weak, women, minorities, and the poor.

In Pakistan, religion is used blatantly for short-term gains even by the supposedly enlightened and mainstream political parties. In India, this is not the case with all mainstream parties; but the ones which use religion and are also mainstream do it no less blatantly than their Pakistani counterparts to arouse negative emotions among their constituents. I acknowledge that due to the secular nature of its Constitution, the Indian state has a somewhat different character in many ways. And there have been no dictatorships there either. However some significant and influential parts of Indian society demonstrate their parochial character from time to time. The Muslim minority in India has seen massive riots and faced loot and murder since 1947, from Muradabad to Ahmedabad to Mumbai to now Muzaffarnagar in the recent past. The Christian minority has been persecuted. What happened to the Sikhs in the aftermath of Indira

Gandhi's assassination in 1984 is known to all. All over Punjab, Sikhs had sided with Hindus at the time of Partition in 1947 and took part in horrible acts of brutality and violence. Bangladesh is fast catching up with India and Pakistan in being brutal and vindictive. While it was important to establish responsibility and identify and try those who they see as having been collaborators of the Pakistan Army in the 1971 liberation war, but like the rest of South Asians, they could not find the courage to have a process of truth and reconciliation similar to that in South Africa or Ireland. They could not move on. After more than forty-one years, they have started sentencing old people to death. At the same time, there is no recognition of the atrocities Bihari or West Pakistani civilians were subjected to by Bangladeshi freedom fighters. Even if the atrocities were much smaller in magnitude than those the West Pakistani Army carried out, the truth has to be established. The Bangladeshi state also wishes to subsume small ethnic or political identities in the name of nationalism, like the Pakistani state wishes to subsume all different identities in the name of Islam.

Therefore, South Asian societies need a lot of soul searching and our states must set the course right by taking tangible steps to build a shared social interest, create a common market of commodities, and encourage labour exchange while each retains its territorial sovereignty. Dreaming of peace and romanticizing inherent humanity amongst South Asians will not suffice. Unless the governments, military, media, and the people of India and Pakistan are not willing to imagine a different South Asia and understand what Ustani Ji understood, there will be more blood, more chaos, more suffering, and more pain.

****

As a child I was being taught to read the Quran in Arabic by a seasoned tutor. Her name was Husna but she was called Ustani Ji by all and sundry. Whatever little I learned in terms of content had to come through translations later in life, but I am grateful to Ustani Ji for helping initiate my interest in the depth and vastness of scriptures, the sense of rhythm and revolution, metaphor and simile, diction and style. Learning to read the Quran improved my understanding of the Urdu script which I was struggling to learn at school. But what I also truly learnt from her was respect for pluralism and a deep sense of compassion for humanity at large. For her, that is what the Quran stood for, despite all she had gone through during the Partition of India and her migration to Pakistan in the name of religion.

Ustani Ji was a teenager when her family was forced to migrate from an eastern district of Punjab to Pakistan. Most families who were not privileged enough to reach Delhi and fly out to Karachi were looted, abducted, raped, and killed on the way. Ustani Ji had an elder brother who was already working in Sukkur, a city in the province of Sindh, which had become a part of Pakistan. He went to the Lahore railway station to receive his family arriving from India on a special train bringing refugees from East Punjab. What he found was a wagon full of thirty-six corpses, including that of his mother. The only person alive was his younger sister, who miraculously survived the carnage, hidden under the dead bodies that heaped over her one by one. She was traumatized and would never stop crying, even after being married off by her brother to a remote relative of theirs in Karachi. Her husband was a man of simple means but a gentle soul who, on her insistence, took her for Hajj. She once told me that her wounds began to heal when, during Hajj, she saw her mother in a dream asking her to move on with her life.

Ustani Ji came back from Hajj with both tranquillity and sanity restored. She now wanted to find some remunerative work and wished to support her husband, who she dearly loved and respected. Her children were growing up and she had started teaching them to read the Quran. Someone then suggested that that she teach other children and charge them a fee. Ustani Ji was quite old when we met her, but she kept active and said her prayers so many times in a day that nobody could keep count. She fasted for three consecutive months in a year and for six days after Eid ul-Fitr. She was strict in her instruction of the Quran but never forced any of her students or the people she met into believing and practising what she considered necessary for herself, be it faith or rituals. She would never utter a despicable word against the Sikhs or the Hindus, who had massacred thirty-six members of her immediate and extended family in front of her eyes. Many of her neighbours in the Ranchore Lines neighbourhood of Karachi were low caste Hindus whose children she would feed as they never had enough. She played with them in her spare time. When I look back and reflect, I think when Ustani Ji decided to move on and shed her grief, she also decided to shed her anger.

2

Sweat

We must live as if we will never die
— Nazim Hikmet

DID THEY FAIL WHO CHAMPIONED SOCIALIST ECONOMIC IDEALS
and liberal political values in Pakistan during its early years? We can
say that the penalty they paid is heavy. They faced persecution and
were treated shabbily by the state during their political struggle, before
their dream of an egalitarian world was rejected, in some sense, by
the very people who they had sacrificed for. And the recognition and
reward for their struggle is of little consequence. The respect and
reverence accorded to them, by a few admirers from later generations,
has little meaning in the larger scheme of things. In retrospect, was all
that a sheer waste of time and space, of verve and vivacity, to follow
these socialist ideologues and leaders in Pakistan—from Dada Amir
Haider and Sobho Gyanchandani to Imam Ali Nazish and Ghaus
Bux Bizenjo?

With a smugness that characterizes either young age or an early
brush with limited knowledge, I had put these questions about the
failure of the socialist movement in Pakistan to Dr Aizaz Nazeer when
I last met him in 1998. The arch revolutionary and one of the earliest
trade unionists in the country, Nazeer had spent decades in prison
while fighting the martial rules of Generals Ayub, Yahya, and Zia
from 1958 to 1988. Zulfikar Ali Bhutto, Pakistan's elected president/
prime minister (1972–77), also kept Nazeer behind bars for quite
some time. However, after Bhutto's hanging, which is commonly

termed as judicial murder under General Zia ul-Haq, by his party supporters and democrats alike, Nazeer stood by Bhutto's wife Nusrat and daughter Benazir in the struggle for the restoration of democracy and political freedom during the martial law period of General Zia ul-Haq. Dr Aizaz Nazeer took my question about the failure of socialist movement with great poise. Rather than being defensive and telling me that some stalwarts like himself and Abid Hasan Minto in ideological parties, and Aitzaz Ahsan and Afrasiab Khattak in popular parties are still fighting it out in the face of all odds, he plainly said that the socialist revolution he and his companions believed in never came about. The Soviet Union disintegrated and China is changing its course to a market economy. Therefore one can say that the movement he was a part of did not succeed. He stated with a lot of confidence that the movement will succeed eventually but not in his lifetime. But the way in which his leaders and his own comrades brought compassion for humanity into our social consciousness and body politic must not be undermined. The socialist movement impacted political values and personal choices for hundreds of thousands of women and men in Pakistan. With a big grin on his face he said that maybe they could have done better, but he is not apologetic. He and his comrades always sided with the weak and changed the way people like me would forever view this world.

Fatehyab Ali Khan held the same opinion when the same question was posed to him. He was a student leader in the 1950s and the 1960s, led civil and political movements and joined the Pakistan Workers Party, which was later merged into the Mazdoor Kissan Party (MKP). He was among the twelve prominent student activists exiled from Sindh when they pioneered a movement against General Ayub's martial law in the 1960s. He remained associated with the MKP as its main leader until his death in 2013. He played a major convening role during the Movement for the Restoration of Democracy (MRD) against General Zia ul-Haq and championed the rights of workers and peasants all his life with remarkable conviction.

I recall one downcast evening in the violence ridden Karachi of the 1990s when some of my friends and acquaintances were discussing the shortcomings of Leftist politics in Pakistan, in architect Arif Hasan's living room. A verbal attack was launched on Fatehyab Ali Khan, as the only former stalwart of the socialist movement present in that company. Someone provoked him by saying that to attend a conference of political parties held some years ago, Khan's MKP couldn't even find three delegates to send. Fatehyab Ali Khan remained unflustered. He calmly said that on that day, it was hard to find a third delegate who could represent them. But they always have a principled position and that, in his view, matters no less. He wanted radical changes in the way things are run in Pakistan, but believed in constitutionalism and filed a number of historic petitions which left a mark on the political history of the country. He relentlessly pursued cases for the realization of fundamental rights. He believed that a time will come when millions of people will desire to become the third member of his delegation that will represent the values of equality, justice, and human dignity.

****

People like Dr Aizaz Nazeer and Fatehyab Ali Khan were not quite as common as bread. Yet they were in significant number dedicated fully to their cause, and excelling in whichever fields they chose for themselves. Some may still be alive but most are not. I call them the quiet rebels of early Pakistan who were born in the 1920s and the 1930s. They were sophisticated non-conformists. A generation of dreamers who believed in working hard to make their dreams come true and never gave up.

One such person was Ahmad Bashir. In 1976 when Jinnah's centenary was being celebrated in Pakistan, he was tasked as the Chairman of State Film Authority to produce a film on the founder of the nation. As the producer, he commissioned the arch progressive writer and intellectual Safdar Mir to pen the script and convinced my father to direct the film. He contracted my father who was deputed from the Department of Films and Publications to work for Bashir on the project. All three of them were known to each other from their days in Mumbai when they had arrived together from Lahore some time before Partition. They may have had minor political differences but shared an overall view of the world. The film, titled *Quaid-i-Azam*, was released in December 1976 at the fag end of the PPP's first government. In July 1977, as soon as Zulfikar Ali Bhutto was deposed by General Zia ul-Haq, the film was banned. They had no other option but to scrap it because there could have been a worst possible combination of a producer, scriptwriter, and director put together by an eager to be progressive state of Pakistan of the 1970s to make a film on its founder. Progressivism was short-lived. Of course, Jinnah was depicted in the film as they viewed him to be—a modern, secular constitutionalist and democrat.

Once I accompanied the film unit to watch the shooting of *Quaid-i-Azam*. There were four people carrying heavy equipment. They camped in the middle of the gardens on the southern side of the mausoleum. They had been told by Ahmad Bashir, earlier in the day, that he would meet them at the mausoleum but he was nowhere to be found. There were no cell phones then and we had to physically search for Bashir in the expansive grounds of the mausoleum of Quaid-i-Azam Mohammad Ali Jinnah.

It was a warm evening and we had been looking for Bashir for quite some time when we decided to ask one of the caretaker staff at the mausoleum if he had seen a man of such and such appearance in or around the mausoleum. He told us that there was a man sleeping on the stairs for some time on the eastern side but it seemed unlikely that he would be the one we were looking for as he did not look like a filmmaker by any means. We hurriedly climbed up the stairs and then climbed down from the other side. There we saw a man sleeping in a crumpled, yellow kurta-shalwar. He had taken off his sandals and kept them by the side of his head covered in a newspaper—a precautionary measure, perhaps, so that no one nicked his footwear. When my father shook him lightly by his shoulder, he first tried to turn to the other side but since it was a narrow space he had to get up. He embraced my father and apologized. He said he was too tired and could not help dozing off. Being the head of a major government institution at that time had not changed the simple ways which he had acquired as a socialist political worker, committed journalist, and experimental filmmaker.

After retirement from filmmaking, Ahmad Bashir's remarkable pen portraits in Urdu, *Jo Miley Thay Raastey Mein*, were published and widely appreciated. His autobiographical novel, *Dil Bhatkey Gaa*, appeared a few years later. It was in early 2001 that I invited him to attend my father's seventy-fifth birthday, meant to be a surprise for him from his friends and family. Ahmad Bashir, who was himself seventy-eight and not enjoying good health, came all the way from Lahore to Karachi just to make an old friend feel important. Three years later he passed away after living a full-blooded life with honour and integrity, siding with the weak and speaking out for the dispossessed. When someone haughtily declares today that the struggle between the Right and the Left is over, I remember people like him. His commitment to socialism was undeterred and he lived a simple life. His appointment to senior management positions by the government was always expected to be a short stint.

Some other people from the same ilk as Bashir's who I was privileged to meet and spend time with were journalists, poets, scholars, and trade unionists like Rafiq Jabir, Wahid Bashir and his wife Hamza Wahid, Anwar Ahsan Siddiqui, Dr Mohammed Ali Siddiqui, Faqir Mohammed Lashari, and Professor Hasan Abid. All have passed away, and with them the deep-rooted organized relationship between literati and labour in Pakistan virtually came to an end. The progressive trade union movement in Pakistan partly owes its downfall to liberalization and deregulation of the economy by the elite-captured state and partly due to the intellectual disassociation and cynicism of Pakistani thinkers and writers.

In 2008, one such trade unionist and political worker from that generation who passed away unsung, uncelebrated, and in oblivion in a modest dwelling in Kot Lakhpat, Lahore, was Manzoor Ahmed. He was born in a village in the Vehari district of Punjab. His career as a teenage political worker began with chanting slogans and organizing meetings for Zulfikar Ali Bhutto and the PPP in the 1960s. He was once badly beaten and his arms broken by some people, including his co-workers acting on behalf of the management of Ittefaq Foundries, where he was employed in Lahore. He later became a member of Muttahida Mazdoor Majlis-i-Amal (United Labour Action Committee), one of the largest trade unions in the country and the predecessor of the Muttahida (United) Labour Federation. Much before the emergence of the full-fledged Movement for Restoration of Democracy (MRD) in 1983, General Zia ul-Haq and his coterie started muffling any voice which was raised against their autocracy and state-sponsored terrorism. Manzoor became a part of the newly formed Punjab Lok Party and was arrested in June 1980 on the charge of possessing and distributing pamphlets called *Jamhoori Pakistan, Gajar,* and *Chanan.* Before being tried for sedition against the state of Pakistan in a military court and kept in Camp Jail, Lahore, he was first taken to the debriefing and torture cells of Lal Qila, Waris Road, and finally the notorious Shahi Qila. He was kept awake for sixteen days and sixteen nights. When they failed to break his will, he was hung from the hook of a ceiling fan in the cell, with chains and bar fetters squeezing his arms and legs, and an iron yoke bolted around his neck. Besides inflicting terrible physical pain, this brutality caused permanent damage to his spine and nervous system. His condition started to deteriorate and in a few years he became completely immobile. He was unable to move his hands and the lower parts of his legs for years.

Being found innocent, the court released Manzoor Ahmed after two-and-a-half years. But a few years after his own release, paying no heed to his failing health, in 1987 he organized a grand reception for Jam Saqi, another famous political prisoner from Sindh, who was visiting Lahore. About the same time, Manzoor opened a small shop selling *paan*, cigarettes, chewing tobacco, and candy to run his household and to provide for not only his own, but his brother's family as well. He never asked any of his friends for support and ran his small shop with dignity. Manzoor Ahmed was one of the many political workers who, irrespective of their affiliations, gave meaning to the struggle for a just and prosperous country. It is ironic that there were only twenty people in the graveyard to pay their last respects to him when he died.

****

Not all died as completely unsung heroes. Some belonging to Manzoor Ahmed's larger movement were recognized by their comrades and friends. One reason may be that they belonged to the educated middle class and had access to media and social networks. But that cannot be held against them as they dedicated their lives to Left-wing politics and labour movements, or were members of the Progressive Writers Association if they were poets or writers, or the Indian People's Theatre Association if actors and dramatists before 1947. Zamir Niazi and Mahmood Faridoon were among such people.

Zamir Niazi made a name for himself as the chronicler of Pakistan's press, censorship, coercion, and freedom of expression. I used to visit him every Sunday for years and find him sitting on his bed, encircled by books and newspapers, holding a pen and paper clipped on to a hardboard, busy taking notes or writing something. His first book, *Press in Chains,* appeared as soon as Prime Minister Mohammad Khan Junejo had lifted the state of emergency before he himself was ousted by General Zia. After completing his first book, Niazi wrote and dictated more books, the most notable being: *Press*

Under Siege, The Web of Censorship, and *Hikayat-i-Khoon Chakaan* (in Urdu while sitting like that for a number of years). He had developed a cancer of the colon and could not sit properly. Either he had to lie down on one side or squat in a certain way. I met everyone from the owners and publishers of the media industry like Hameed Haroon and M. A. Zuberi to editors and columnists like Rehana Hakim and Ardeshir Cowasjee here. Niazi was a professional journalist who met people from all walks of life espousing all kinds of beliefs and supporting all types of political positions.

Until the 1980s and early 1990s, there were three functional ideological camps among the journalists, so to speak. First type included the Z. A. Suleri and Majeed Nizami-type Muslim Leaguers; second were those who were influenced by the Jamaat-i-Islami; and the third were those who belonged to the Left. The groups would contest each other at the level of ideas as well as fighting turf wars when it came to matters of their unions and press clubs. Although this acrimony would rarely translate into personal feuds, the social and political circle in which people like us grew up would reject Suleri and his like for the positions they took on issues faced by the Pakistani state and society and brand them as 'reactionary', 'pro-establishment', or 'Right-wing'.

One such 'Right-winger' to be found in Niazi's company was Abul Akhyar. Once a close associate of the conservative journalist of yesteryear, Z. A. Suleri, and a deeply conservative man himself when it came to religion and politics, I was told that he rejected Leftist politics and ideological views with a conviction. But at a personal and professional level, he remained close and dear to Leftist stalwarts in Karachi like Anis Hashmi, Dr Ashraf, Zamir Niazi, and Wahid Bashir.

When I was assisting Zamir Niazi in compiling a book of his writings in Urdu, *Hikayat-i-KhoonChakaan*, I remember meeting Akhyar on a number of occasions since he visited Niazi regularly. Irrespective of their political differences, Zamir Niazi would discuss and review his findings, analysis, and the chronology of events mentioned in his book at length with Akhyar. Abul Akhyar was a journalist first and foremost—a dedicated professional who would speak the truth about an event or a happening and restrain himself and others from giving an unwanted, prejudiced spin of personal views when he was reporting or editing. He would not reject the fact if it challenged his faith. He may analyse the cause differently.

Abul Akhyar was tough on novices on the desk and in the newsroom. When my younger brother joined the daily *Business Recorder*, Akhyar asked him and another two colleagues of his who were fresh, to sit in his room for two months and report directly to him. 'They don't teach you anything in college or university these days and I am going to make you learn,' Akhyar was categorical. For two months he grilled them relentlessly. My brother tells me that he would do the same with everyone and put in much time and energy into making young people learn the profession. I remember Niazi and Akhyar together for their professionalism and human values.

Mahmood Faridoon had known Zamir Niazi and my father from their days in Mumbai during the late 1940s. He would spend a lot of time at our place in the 1980s and worked with my father on different films and film publication projects. He was always carrying a black briefcase full of files and papers with defective locks and loose hinges. A little older than my father, he had been the General Secretary of M. N. Roy's Radical Socialist Party in Punjab during his youth. He was a committed Marxist who spent all his life struggling for labour rights besides trying to make films and write plays. His drama, 'Murder of Bhutto', was well received in those times. It was an act of great courage to say the least. He then moved to Sweden to live with his sons. I remember he would write letters to us and once asked my father to send me to study in Sweden as the education was free and I could live with his family for as long as I wished.

A truly memorable event for me is when I escorted Faridoon and my father to meet arch poet Faiz Ahmed Faiz. It was 1982. The place was Begum Amina Majeed Malik's drawing room in Karachi.

Mahmood Faridoon was editing a publication on film and television and wanted Faiz to write a dedicated piece for that anthology. Faiz, as many would know, indulged in films as much as in other fields of art and culture. I may have already met him as a child, but since I started reading his work this was my first meeting. Unfortunately, it also happened to be the last. One can very well imagine how excited a young teenager with a keen interest in literature and politics would feel meeting the most celebrated poet, educationist, trade unionist, political worker, champion of the rights of the wretched of the earth, and the greatest living literary and cultural icon of the country.

I listened intently as Begum Majeed Malik and three others settled down to discuss contemporary politics of the times and Zia's martial rule, the situation in Palestine and Lebanon, the difficult times faced by artists, writers, and journalists in Pakistan, and the possibility of a return to the democratic order. I crouched in a deep leather sofa by the window of that enormous drawing room. Faiz would keep clearing his throat and struggled while speaking. Finally, he asked Begum Majeed Malik, his host, for a cough syrup. Oblivious while dropping it on the thick carpet and leaving stains, which could have been permanent, he kept pouring the syrup again and again into a small spoon and sipped from it until the bottle was almost done. He finished the bottle in fifteen minutes, if not ten. Then he asked for some paper and took less than half an hour to write in long hand a piece for Faridoon's film and television anthology. After he was done they all began to chat again. Faiz then turned his head towards me while asking my father if his son could make coffee. I nodded and walked up to the trolley sitting in the middle of the room. Faridoon was quickly reading through Faiz's piece while also participating in the conversation. He politely intervened when I was in the middle of asking how Faiz liked his coffee. Faridoon complimented Faiz for his command over English idiom. Faiz looked at me again at that point while telling Faridoon that our children studying only English is not good enough. They should learn English but must know their own language as well. He then related an incident, which I have quoted before in a couple of my pieces on mother tongues and language issues in Pakistan.

Faiz told us that once he had to travel to Moscow via Delhi because there were no direct flights from Pakistan to the then USSR. After dinner at a senior Pakistani diplomat's residence in Delhi, the diplomat's son asked Faiz for an autograph. Faiz inscribed one of his verses and put his signature. The boy looked at his autograph book in amazement and told Faiz that he knew such good English and his father had told him that Faiz was also the editor of a leading newspaper, but he had given him the autograph in their cook's language. Begum Amina Majeed Malik told me then that I must listen to what Faiz has just said.

****

Begum Majeed Malik, with a passion for art and literature was not just a patron of literature and literary writers as many have come to think of her due to her association with Faiz. She herself was an ardent believer in socialism. I recall visiting her a few times during my childhood with my father, much like the day when Faiz was staying at her place. We also kept meeting her at literary functions and book launches. She used to spend considerable amounts of time at Ghalib Library in Karachi when it was being established by Mirza Zafar-ul-Hasan and his associates while heading the *Idara-i-Yadgar-i-Ghalib*, an institution dedicated to the promotion of Mirza Ghalib's work. She would also come to the premieres of my father's documentary films. There was some familial connection between her and my father through a family marriage two generations ago and she would always fondly mention that relationship to people who were strangers to my father.

Begum Amina Majeed Malik was an eminent educationist and established the PECHS Girls School and PECHS Girls College in Karachi. They were nationalized by the government and then later named after her. My mother once told me an interesting incident about her appearing for an interview for a lectureship position in the PECHS College before she had married my father. It was the early 1960s and the interviewers happened to be Faiz Ahmed Faiz and Begum Amina Majeed Malik. Begum Majeed Malik was very kind and considerate but my mother, who did not recognize Faiz that day and he did not introduce himself, thought that the gentleman spoke very decently but somehow looked intoxicated. She always laughed and told my father that she decided not to take the job because of the way Faiz looked that day.

Another interesting anecdote about Begum Majeed Malik related to me by my mentor in community development, Sadiqa Salahuddin, is about a woman lecturer who had fallen in love. She came to Begum Majeed Malik crying and said that she has a husband and children but she had fallen head over heels in love with another man. She wanted to leave her husband and marry that man but was terribly confused and sought guidance. Begum Majeed Malik told her in a dry, matter of fact manner that there is nothing wrong with falling in love. And that she is sure that the young lecturer will keep falling in love again and again for many more years. However, she cannot keep marrying a new person each time she falls in love.

****

Someone with a similar, dry humour like that of Begum Majeed Malik was a leading lawyer in Karachi, Syed Izhar Haider Rizvi. He overwhelmed people around him with his depth of knowledge and upright disposition. I haven't seen a man more candid, frank, straightforward, and honest than Rizvi in dealing with both people and situations. He also motivated my father to write about his days in Lucknow, Lahore, and Mumbai and record an independent history of the Progressive Writer's Association. Besides being a practising lawyer and an author who wrote a large number of law books in Urdu, he was an engaging conversationalist.

Rizvi called himself a 'former socialist' and said that he had learnt the hard way that in any person, character is more important than ideology. Upon being asked why he had settled for being a former socialist, and whether he now believed in an unregulated and free market economy, he would say that he did not. But after Hasan Nasir and Nazeer Abbasi, who laid their lives for the socialist movement in Pakistan, he could not see many who had that same courage and character.

Hasan Nasir was a member of the central committee of the then proscribed Communist Party of Pakistan, and a bright, young leader of the working class movement who was tortured to death in 1960 under General Ayub Khan's martial law. Nasir was 32. His body was exhumed but remained unrecognizable due to brutal torture marks. He was reburied by the police in a hitherto unknown grave in Lahore. Nasir was quoted by another veteran leader Major (retd.) Mohammad Ishaq as saying upon his return, 'I went to India, but after my exile I came back. My family's lands and riches could not keep me there. Neither could the party; my family had spoken to them that I should work there... But that is not where my struggle is. The labourers I have lived with, learnt from, and taught socialism to—they are here, in Karachi. Not in India. This is why I came here, so will you. Our graves will be made in this land.' His grave ended up being in the heart of this land—Lahore. His wish was granted by Ayub's junta, but perhaps a little too soon.

Nazeer Abbasi, who followed in the footsteps of Hasan Nasir, was killed twenty years after Nasir in 1980 at the age of twenty-eight. Hailing from Tando Allahyar, a small town in the southern part of the Sindh province, he was barely nineteen when he helped organize a municipal workers union in his native town. Abbasi participated in and led students, workers, peasants, and language rights movements. He was the youngest member of the central committee of the Communist Party of Pakistan at the time of his death. He was sent to prison a number of times between 1978 and 1980 before finally being picked up by the Field Intelligence Unit of the martial law regime of General Zia ul-Haq, tortured, and subsequently killed.

Rizvi, an ardent admirer of Nasir and Abbasi, would come visit my parents every Sunday morning for years without fail. He had a penchant for classical Urdu and Persian poetry. Like Syed Izhar Haider Rizvi, I am also learning as I grow older that most of the time the character of a person is more important than their ideology.

****

Three extraordinary men of impeccable character from that generation, who were the beacons of progressive thought and literature in Islamabad—a city which was otherwise hugely intellectually challenged—were Dr Aftab Ahmad Khan, Sadiq Hussain, and Professor Khawaja Masud.

Dr Aftab Ahmad Khan spent his life as a senior civil servant but his love for Ghalib and passion for Urdu poetry became his claim to fame. Like Ahmad Bashir, his reflections on people who attracted or influenced him, titled *Bayad-i-Sohbat-i-Nazuk Khayalaan*, is critically acclaimed. He wrote a number of other books on Urdu poets and poetry. Khan was the one who had commissioned my father to make a film on the life and work of Ghalib when he was the Information Secretary of the Government of Pakistan. I would sometimes meet Dr Khan in his cosy study where we would have tea and a session on Ghalib's Persian verse.

Sadiq Hussain for the most part of his professional career remained a senior company executive before becoming an adviser to some leading corporate firms. For five decades or more he wrote remarkable short stories in Urdu. My father was not an expressive man but never concealed his fondness for Sadiq Hussain's person and his literary talent. What a pity that they could not meet for years before each of them passed away a thousand miles apart. I saw him more in his last years than my father could. He told me about his time in East

Pakistan and the way he viewed the divide between the western and eastern wings of Pakistan. Once, Hussain recalled an incident from some years after the fall of Dhaka when he was sitting in the famous Shezan Restaurant, Dayal Singh Mansion, Lahore. An army officer from his village near Murree, who had retired by then, was sitting with him and a few others, including Lt General Niazi. The officer made some abhorrent comments about Bangladeshi women and Pakistan army men. Hussain apparently felt so infuriated with the meanness of that man that he started swearing at him and was about to hit him on his face when others intervened. He said that the Germans and Japanese had learnt from their humiliating defeats in the Second World War and that is the reason they became great powers again. We do not wish to learn from any of our blunders and will never rise unless we do.

Once, during tea at his place, perhaps on my last visit before his death he told me that my father and he had never believed in the occult or supernatural happenings, but there is something that he wanted to tell me. I became a little curious and thought that something really uncanny is about to be shared. Then he said that whenever dry *dhuli maash ki dal*, the white lentils my father loved, were cooked in Hussain's home my father would somehow arrive at the dinner table. It happened year after year and so many times that first his eldest daughter and then others started noticing the unique occurrence. 'There was definitely something supernatural there,' he said. He also recollected how before my father was married, Hussain insisted that my aunt, my father's sister, cook him *arhar ki dal* (yellow lentils) and not the usual meat dishes whenever he visited them in Karachi. So we were *maash-arhar bhai*, brothers-in-lentils; he looked at me and smiled. He was frail and I did not want him to come out to see me off, but not only did he insist, he also walked with me until the end of the street where someone was waiting to pick me up, and then turned back with his arm in the air, waving at me.

Sadiq Hussain travelled the world and across Pakistan for his professional work. He wrote short stories that were read and enjoyed by many. The part of the country where Islamabad is located was Sadiq Hussain's ancestral home base for centuries. Some of his stories capture the life and livelihood of common women and men of the Potohar Plateau—Rawalpindi and its adjoining cities, towns, and villages—and the Murree Hills where Hussain belonged.

But in the times I mention, someone who became the guru of the twin cities of Rawalpindi-Islamabad, a mentor and a teacher, an ideologue and a visionary, a writer and a commentator, a household name and a role model, was Professor Khawaja Masud. He and some others like him taught us to claim Pakistan for its citizens and continue to wage the struggle in favour of the powerless. According to people like Khawaja Masud, it is the only choice left for those who refuse to cut their umbilical cord from Pakistan. During his illustrious career as a teacher, Masud taught with equal passion within and outside his classroom. His writings were not only educative but infused a new hope in the future of humanity in the moments you would read or hear him, even if you did not believe it afterwards due to the adverse conditions in which we live. I remember reading him regularly when he wrote a column for *The News International* for some years. It was called 'Feuilleton'. Meeting Khawaja Masud was easier once I had moved to Islamabad. He would come to many public functions in the city and captivate the audiences, sometimes with his fiery speeches and sometimes through his cold historic logic. Knowing my literary and political association with his old comrade, Amin Mughal, he would tell me many interesting things from their shared past. It was a privilege when he chaired the launch of a collection of my English poetry.

When Professor Khawaja Masud passed away in 2010, the cities of Rawalpindi and Islamabad were deep in mourning. His politics and person, writing and conversations, had helped me like so many others to nurture an unbreakable bond with Pakistan. I mentioned in his obituary that he did not want me to leave the dodgy lift that saved me from climbing the stairs in the block of flats where I then lived. It was cranky, shook the passengers enough to scare the faint-hearted, and sometimes just stopped at its will without a reason, technical or otherwise. Unlike other lifts in the building, it continuously exhaled the smell of rusted metal chains, pulleys, and clasps, daubed with grease and some strong lubricating oil. I would still step into it to get straight to my flat. This lift needed maintenance and servicing, its worn-out parts changed, its panel upgraded, and its doors aligned. But the lift could not be abandoned for it was the closest and the cosiest lift. It just had to be fixed.

****

Back in 1995, when I went to work in the UK, Rahat Saeed, who was visiting from Pakistan, brought Professor Amin Mughal to meet me. My father had already mentioned a few times that Mughal was someone to meet in London. Rahat Saeed is one of the founding editors of *Irtiqa*, the quarterly journal in Urdu promoting progressive political writing, social history, and literature published from Karachi for the last thirty years. He has played a major role in reviving and reorganizing writers within Pakistan and other developing countries. He and Mughal started coming to my place every evening in that winter of 1995 for as long as Saeed was present in London on that trip. After moving to the UK in 1984, Mughal has not returned to Pakistan once. My father only came on one occasion to spend some time in the UK in 1999, around the time I was finishing my degree programme. That is when the two of them connected and met as if they went to school together, although Mughal is much younger than my father. The former Leftist leader, political worker, and office bearer of the Progressive Writers Association, Hameed Akhtar, was also in London in 1999. The three of them came together once and discussed the history and politics of the South Asian subcontinent. I wish that day-long conversation could have been recorded for posterity.

Mughal used to put up with the hide-and-seek played between the governments and Leftist political activists during the 1960s and the 1970s, sporting frequent arrests, or minor jail terms. But seven years into General Zia's repressive martial law, he was faced with a singular choice: leave quietly or get lashed publicly on some trumped-up charge. Working initially as a journalist and political commentator in London, he retired to voluntary social service in his neighbourhood hospital. He hosts guests of all hues and colours from Pakistan. A voracious reader and a keen observer of life in general, and politics in particular, he is undoubtedly one of the most ardent thinkers from Pakistan. He did not put himself to writing a book but his intellectual prowess and understanding of world politics is unmatched, reflected in his talks, papers, and informal conversations. Mughal and his like personify the conscience of a nation. They condemn, reject, and disapprove of the state and society to which they belong out of one single belief: that the suffering of humanity must end and a new era of prosperity for all must begin. It seems as if some leave home out of deliberate choice, but if truth be told, their native country drives them out. The intolerance shown towards dissent in Pakistani society through bombs, bullets, petty actions, or caustic words is comparable to very few other places in the world. Nevertheless, such people remain loyal to their habitat and bewail like a crane separated from its flock.

****

These women and men who represented the progressive movement mark an age. I have not seen such people in the generation that succeeded them however, exceptions may exist. One may continue to argue if they failed or succeeded. But they never gave up on their fight for Nasir Khan and the likes of him.

Nasir Khan hailed from Mardan. He was four when he moved to Karachi with his family. He grew up there, chewing *paan* and spitting out the red saliva like his other mates, drinking strong tea, sharing jokes in a cranky voice, and playing cricket with an old bat with nails hammered into it and a tennis ball wrapped with plastic tape. He sold hairpins and waistbands in the Nazimabad Chowrangi market and spoke the city's colloquial working-class Urdu. He attended a municipality-run school with yellow walls and dingy rooms for five years. That made him literate and numerate. He also went to the local mosque for some years to learn to read the Quran. His father was a little irregular in these matters but his mother would always ask her son to go to the school and mosque.

At the age of nineteen, Khan got married to a seventeen-year-old cousin. They started producing children right away as was the tradition. Khan himself had six siblings, his wife had eight. Khan's father, after working for several years as a labourer at the Karachi port, settled as a small vegetable vendor who would pull his cart for hours incessantly in the relatively middle-class neighbourhoods within the Nazimabad and North Nazimabad areas, which were not very far away from Khan's own neighbourhood of Pak Colony. As he grew older, Nasir Khan helped his father sell vegetables in addition to his own vending. But soon he graduated from selling hairpins to driving a rickshaw. He was first trained and then hired by a local rickshaw owner, who happened to be his elder sister's father-in-law, plying the roads of Karachi for fourteen hours a day. This increased his income considerably; and from a gross income of five thousand rupees a month, he started earning an average twelve thousand rupees in a month. Swiftly, the family married off Khan's younger sister.

Nasir Khan's father had a road accident soon after, and stayed bedridden for more than six months. The family spent everything they had on his treatment—from selling his vegetable cart to some family utensils they owned. He finally passed away in misery. This happened two years after Khan had started his rickshaw job and not only did his increased income deplete fast, he also came under a debt amounting to hundreds of thousands of rupees due to his father's illness and the much needed medicines, food, and occasional hospitalization expenses. Although they used to go to a government health facility, just the cab fare to and from the hospital would cost them a few hundred rupees. Khan worked extra hours without a break and would ask every passenger who hired his rickshaw for some extra money. He started eating at a shrine where free food was served, restricted his tea habit to two cups a day, not buying even a low-cost shalwar kameez for two years, he eventually cleared all his debt.

Nasir Khan had five children when he died in a government hospital at the age of twenty-nine. He had a wife, mother, and four younger siblings to take care of as well. At the time of his death, he was surrounded by all his siblings, his mother, and wife. That was the only solace for him. The first thought that comes to people's minds today when they hear about Nasir Khan is that this may just be another story of a Pakhtun rickshaw driver killed in Karachi. It is perhaps just another story, but the reasons are different. Nasir Khan was not killed because of his ethnicity. No political party can be blamed for his death. He was not shot down on the orders of a local cleric, or by a militant group, or sectarian outfit. He died of an illness—a very easily treatable stomach ailment. Khan subjected himself to inhumanly hard work in order to feed and support more than ten members of his extended family, send his children to school, and clear the debt the family was burdened with due to his father's injury and long illness. He almost starved himself to save money and drank polluted water from any source he could find. Consequently, he developed a disease in his stomach and intestines. He did not go to the hospital for months and suffered in silence. Neither did he have the money required for his treatment nor the time or luxury to stay away from work.

One night, when Khan was taken to the hospital by his wife and a neighbour after he spat red saliva, he looked pale and scared. This time, the red was not there because of his habit of chewing betel leaves—he was now spitting blood. He was kept there for two days but did not survive. He was an ordinary working-class Pakistani, from among the millions, with no citizenship rights, no economic opportunities, no decent living conditions, no social safety net, no possibility to receive a modern education and the awareness it brings, and no access to respectable health facilities.

Although the progressive movement has diminished in Pakistan and the women and men of yesteryear who espoused socialism are passing into oblivion, there are many who still worry about Nasir Khan. There are many who would find the story of his life noteworthy and newsworthy. But there are few who would stand up for him and practically struggle for his life to be changed. Dr Aizaz Nazeer may well be right in his response to the question about the success or failure of his movement by emphasizing the change in consciousness that was brought about by the socialists in Pakistan. But the incapability of that change in consciousness in transforming society keeps this question valid. Nasir Khan passed away the same year as my father.

****

My father, Khalique Ibrahim Khalique, was my first introduction to the Progressive Writers' Movement and socialist ideology. Pen and clapperboard were his hammer and sickle. Through him, I was introduced to many significant people who played a central role in revolutionary struggles and labour movements. After making Karachi his home town, he had to work—day in and day out—in order to merely survive and support his kin. The bygone affluence of his family and the lost means he once possessed had no bearing on his new life and social imagination.

When my brother and I were growing up, our father was fully consumed by his work—making documentary films on shoestring budgets. Pakistan's government was not as poor and dependent on foreign aid then as it projects itself to be today, but it had the same imports from the beginning. Art and culture were kept on the bottom rung of its priorities. The only use of writers and filmmakers envisioned by the state was to promote and propagate the narrative of the incumbent government, particularly whenever there was a military ruler in power.

There were rapid changes during the 1980s and the 1990s in Pakistan. General Zia ul-Haq's martial law imposed in 1977 was the wrath of God. Its lasting consequences became more evident in the years after it was over. Political workers and journalists suffered the most under Zia. They were lashed publicly, tortured, imprisoned, and killed. Our family was an unhappy witness to that age—just a small victim by the standards of what many other people went through. The documentary films made by my father were censored, banned, remade by other government-appointed directors, or simply shelved.

He had an inalienable connection with nature, universe, humanity, and art. In his view, this was true spirituality. But for the world around him, saying funeral prayers for his relatives and friends was the only ritual they saw him observe. Yet, he celebrated festivals of all kinds with great fervour. When young, I always thought he was confused. But his was a strange sense of identity. He was clear in his own way as he never did anything which he did not believe in. It was quite possible for him to have his staunch belief in socialism exist in complete harmony with his cultural tradition. The privileged in our society want everyone to conform, which my father and his likes from that generation refused to submit to. He would write letters to me when I was away from home. Once he wrote that the pervading atrocities all around did sometimes enervate his senses, causing him to suffer bouts of despair, but despite everything good or bad, the world seemed beautiful and life enchanting.

He used to say that life has to end but I want to live as much as I can. He lived as much as he could. But he wanted to live more and so did I. The final cause of his death was the inability to breathe properly. The body struggled, resisted, fought hard, but eventually fatigued. It was 29 September 2006. When I was a child, whenever we returned home from a funeral, he told me that the body of a dead man is like a grown nail clipped from the finger. It is the work he leaves behind that actually matters. So I should not worry too much about death and its finality. The idea of a grown nail clipped from the finger always consoled me after every funeral I attended, until the day of my father's death. Suddenly it lost its meaning and consolatory effect. I found out that day that my father was wrong. A body of a dead man is not like a nail clipped from a finger. You cannot simply say that the person continues to live in his work and is remembered through his deeds. If you love that woman or man, her/his body is a part of your own flesh and blood, your own sweat and tears; a part of you dies with her/him.

My father's death reminded me of the poem 'Lenox Hill', written by Agha Shahid Ali, the inspiring Kashmiri-American poet of the English language. He wrote for his mother,

'For compared to my grief for you, what are those of Kashmir,
   and what (I close the ledger) are the griefs of the universe...'

3

Tears

Awake upon the darkening land
— Rainer Maria Rilke

LIKE OTHER NATIONS, PAKISTAN PRESENTS A CONTINUING SAGA
of transition—a shift from the past, a migration into the future, and
a transformation from what it was to what it has become and to
what its people wished it to be. What is unique about this journey
Pakistanis take together is that sometimes it feels like they are
moving in the wilderness without knowing where they are headed.
Like a large South Asian train of colonial times with many classes
of travel—Air Conditioned Parlour, First Class, Second Class, and
Economy—lurking on an ancient rail track. Internal struggles are
waged in the underbelly of this collective journey. The less fortunate
passengers wrestle to find more elbow room in the lower classes
of this overcrowded train. Second Class is only marginally better
than Economy. Those who can travel First Class struggle to get a
seat with more leg space. For the rich and the mighty, the ability
to travel while snoozing in a reclining sofa in the Air Conditioned
Parlour behind the engine room tells it as it is. The elite perpetuate.
In many other countries, the elite, even with all its contempt for the
lumpen, would lead and take others along in the wagons behind
them and know where they all are going. In Pakistan, the elite remain
indifferent. Fed and comforted by attendants, they do not seem to
be bothered by the direction the train takes along the track in an
unknown territory.

The plebeian travellers are not served meals. They remain famished, their children malnourished. Food to eat, clothes to wear, a bed to sleep in, a book to read, and a pill to swallow when sick—they struggle for the means to subsist. A five-year-old girl begs for alms and a ten-year-old boy is asked to cook breakfast for older men to get a loaf of bread. An aged brick kiln worker with a wrinkled face stares in awe at those who wear sunshades. Then there are some of the passengers travelling in a better class of the train. Food is served. They get a newspaper to glance at. Still they want more leg space to stretch, not just for the body but for the imagination: the agency to reason, the possibility to question, the freedom to comment, and the ability to reject. They harbour the desire to know where this train is headed. Yet even the existing leg space is being snatched from them. They are denied the leg room that measures up to their height.

Squeezed elbow room and shrinking leg space is the narrative of Pakistan in our times. It is about demanding a dignified physical space to live, a respectable economic space to earn a decent living, a free intellectual space to think, and an uninhibited artistic space to create. Together, it is all about political space. The more I think about it, the more I feel that the assassination of Benazir Bhutto in 2007 was the real watershed in Pakistan's contemporary political history. It has shaken and damaged the polity of Pakistan for a very long time, if not beyond repair. At the societal level, for me, there are five women who characterize this struggle for space for the people of my country, all of whom were born after the creation of Pakistan. Although there are many other women and men who I will mention, these five women somehow define it for me. Three out of these five were shot dead between 2009 and 2015, one lost her son in 2013, and one has been imprisoned since 2009—the last two mentioned are neither dead nor alive in emotional terms. Shabana was killed in 2009 while Aasiya Noreen was sent to jail the same year. Saeeda Bibi's thirty-two-year-old son, Irfan Ali Khudi, was killed in a 2013 bomb blast along with her son-in-law. Perween Rahman was also shot dead in 2013, and Sabeen

Mahmud in 2015. Their stories contain so many other stories, so many other lives, so many other personal histories, and so many other trials and tribulations faced by the ordinary people of Pakistan that if we start writing it all and the ocean were ink, another ocean would have to be added to borrow an expression from a Quranic verse.

****

Let me begin with Shabana, the singer and dancer from Swat. She symbolizes what religious extremism, obscurantism, bigotry, and sectarianism have done to Pakistan. No difference is to be tolerated, no command is to be disobeyed, no other faith is to be practised, and no artist is to perform. Shabana was a dancer of some merit and known in the performing art circles in other parts of the country as well. Before being killed, she begged the men who had dragged her out of the house to not slit her throat, which they would usually do, but shoot her instead. They fulfilled her last wish and shot her in the head. Her corpse was hung from the lamp post like those of other such victims in the main square of the chief city of the Swat Valley in the province of Khyber Pakhtunkhwa where such executions were regularly being carried out. Shabana came from those traditional families in Swat who sing and dance for a living. Over the generations, some of them have been travelling to, and working in, other places including Lahore. They perform at weddings and other joyous occasions and festivals across the region. Shabana had refused to follow the diktat of the Taliban when they were ruling Swat; she had continued performing at public functions and did not stop from training young singers and dancers in her home.

The Swat Valley is one of the most beautiful places in Pakistan with snow-clad mountains laying the backdrop, fresh water streams full of trout that reel along, fruit orchards with apricot and plum-laden trees and, above all, warm, hospitable, welcoming, and industrious people. Swat was dominated and controlled by the Taliban between 2006 and 2009. As a matter of daily routine, they were killing unarmed civilians, political workers of liberal and progressive parties, paramilitary personnel, and journalists that advertently or inadvertently flouted the rules set by them. Schools were blown up and women were not allowed to step out of their houses let alone work outside. The story of young Malala Yousufzai from Swat, Pakistani Nobel Laureate who champions the cause of education for girls, is known to all.

The scintillating valley, that once was the centre of tourism in Pakistan and employed many thousands of people in the hospitality industry, was completely destroyed. It was once a more tolerant and liberal place than many other parts of the country. As a native state, run by a benevolent native ruler during the times of the British, Swat was ahead in both education and prosperity as compared to the other regions surrounding it. Swat stayed the same until a movement led by a local cleric, Sufi Mohammad, jolted it from within in the 1990s and then, finally, when the Taliban took over, it became a flashpoint and a test case for how Islamic extremists will rule Pakistan if they come to power. But how did this extremist political ideology, fortified with violence, come about? It was not an accident. It is a product of the choices that the Pakistani state made at a certain point in time.

Swat saw the rise of Tehrik-i-Nifaz-i-Shariat-i-Mohammadi (TNSM), led by Sufi Mohammad, in the mid-1990s. This group wanted to create a state within a state in the name of faith. In 2008, the same TNSM resurfaced as an amalgam with the Taliban. The authorities certainly looked the other way when dealing with the militants because the Taliban here were linked to the Taliban in Afghanistan, and Pakistan covertly supported certain factions of Afghan Taliban to further its interests in Afghanistan. The government of Pakistan initially made a pact with the new administrators of Swat which was short lived. After signing the agreement, the Taliban announced that their mission was to create a bigger Islamic Emirate and they did not believe in either the political system of democracy or the Constitution of Pakistan. The deal came to an end and the government struck back. Swat saw massive killings of artists, political activists, and liberal and progressive individuals before the government decided to take on the Taliban.

But obscurantism was not limited to Swat or places where the Taliban were in direct control. It was in the week following Eidul Fitr, soon after the Taliban were deposed from Swat, when the Parks and Horticulture Agency in collaboration with the Tourism Development Corporation of Punjab organized the Youth and Family Festival with food, games, shopping, and a host of other activities to entertain people living in and visiting Murree and Bhurban, the hilly and leafy resorts in northern Punjab, during the Eid holidays. The cricket stadium in Bhurban attracted huge numbers on the first day of the festival. There was a free, live music concert planned for the next day. The organizers expected an even bigger turnout as they had widely publicized the event. Popular folk and modern musicians were invited to perform. The news of the concert angered the local clerics. Some approached the organizers and asked them to cancel the event. They were told that it was a part of Eid celebrations to provide entertainment to families that had come from far and wide. The clerics declared that such activities would not be tolerated, there should be a complete ban on such events, and they would make sure that it was called off. They succeeded. Announcements were made on loudspeakers in the whole area and from some local mosques to condemn the music concert as un-Islamic and threats were hurled at the organizers. The government budged.

There was a somewhat similar incident in Karachi in 2013 when, in the heart of a middle-class neighbourhood, a journalist was attacked for watching television and listening to Qawwalis within the confines of his home. If not cosmopolitan, the area can safely be termed a mixed neighbourhood where people belonging to different ethnic and faith groups live. Four men arrived at the house of the journalist, Zainul Abedin. He was roughed up, abused, and threatened with death in front of his younger sister. It was only on the condition that he must never watch television or listen to music that he was spared—for listening to music of any kind is an abominable sin and watching television is forbidden. This proves that what happened in Swat can happen anywhere.

The police, law-enforcing agencies, and even the judiciary either refuse, avoid, or delay taking any action. This inaction of the responsible institutions of the state is a principal reason that the trend of imposing one's belief system over others by force is on the rise. To me, it is not the only concern. There is a penetration of a certain ideology and nurturing of a particular mindset among a number of people in society, some of whom also work for law-enforcing agencies. That makes it complicated and puts the whole system at risk. Most people will budge if the extremists gather a critical mass. There will be a few like Shabana, the singing and dancing woman of Swat, who could not become what the Taliban wanted her to become. She refused to fall in line.

****

Swat is in the north and far away from Quetta, the capital city of the province of Balochistan in the western part of Pakistan. That is where Saeeda Bibi lives. She had no control over her son inheriting the facial features specific to her ethnic clan, the Hazaras. The overwhelming majority of their community belongs to one sect, Shia Islam. Having distinct facial features make them stand out. They speak a dialect of Persian and have been settled in Quetta for centuries. Saeeda Bibi lost her son, Irfan Ali Khudi, in a bomb blast in Quetta in 2013. Her young son-in-law also died in the same blast. She now lives with her widowed daughter.

The Shia-Sunni split in Pakistan has a gruesome history. In the middle and late 1980s, Pakistan was encouraged by the successes of Afghan Mujahideen fighting the Soviets in Afghanistan, who they had nurtured and trained during the Afghan War. They believed that they were now capable of such successes, despite a lack of American assistance, and decided to raise outfits to support the armed struggle in the Indian Punjab and Kashmir. The militant outfits raised for the movement in Kashmir were not supported on the basis of Kashmiri nationalist rights but the rights of Kashmiris as Muslims. They could not have been raised otherwise because a non-Kashmiri could only fight for a Kashmiri on the basis of a shared faith. When you organize people around a faith, they will eventually follow a particular school of thought within that faith. Regrettably, most such outfits became extremist Sunni outfits over the years.

After the toning down of Pakistan's support to the militants struggling for the rights of Kashmiris, these outfits added fuel to the sectarian fire within Pakistan. Also, the Anjuman-i-Sipah-i-Sahaba Pakistan (SSP), committed to converting or eliminating Shia Muslims, was not only allowed to organize and operate, it was encouraged by certain elements to counter the fast popularizing Iranian narrative. Subsequently, Sipah-i-Mohammad was organized by Shias with alleged covert support from Iran to counter-attack Sunni militant outfits. SSP wreaked sectarian havoc across Pakistan before being banned in 2001, along with Sipah-i-Mohammad, by General Pervez Musharraf, another military ruler, interestingly just a little before 9/11. SSP was organized under a new name soon after—Ahle Sunnat Wal Jamaat—with a militant wing, Lashkar-i-Jhangvi, that is supposed to have created links with Jundullah in Iran, the Taliban in Afghanistan and Pakistan, and allegedly, the cells of Al-Qaeda operating in the region. The Shia-Sunni split is countrywide and graffiti against Shias is commonplace. They are killed individually and collectively in Gilgit-Baltistan, Balochistan, Karachi, and some parts of Punjab and Khyber-Pakhtunkhwa after being branded profane and devious. How did we get here?

In 1980, I passed the middle-school examination and entered the ninth grade. Imparting school education to children was not as commercialized across the country as it is now. The public schools were far more multi-class in terms of their student strength as well. My school was initially run by the Cantonment and Garrison Educational Institutions which later merged into the Federal Government Educational Institutions (FGEI). My school mates came from varying social strata and different ethnic backgrounds. It was considered normal, at least in my school, that the son of a serving Brigadier shared his desk, books, food, and sporting gear with the son of a non-commissioned officer or soldier. Children who had come from civilian families could be very rich or just plain middle class. The divisions of such nature were played down by the school administration and teachers. The culture that prevailed in the classroom, library, hockey field, and cricket ground was inclusive, largely egalitarian, and merit-based.

The divisions of ethnic, sectarian, or religious nature among students in the secondary school were mostly invisible. Although there were some Christian boys studying with us, and maybe a few from other faiths, the differences were seldom highlighted. Besides, some of our teachers also belonged to other faiths. Boys in the school would fight among themselves, as naturally happens with boys that age, but even when enraged, there were never insinuations to the adversary's social background, language, or faith by either of the fighting parties. We were all equal, or at least the school was successful in creating that illusion among its students.

The first significant division introduced officially among the ranks of the students came when we reached the ninth grade. While a couple of non-Muslim students opted for ethics as a subject, Islamiat was a compulsory subject for Muslim students. We were given a choice to opt for either Sunni Islamiat or Shia Islamiat. This was during the prime of General Zia ul-Haq's martial rule. He had begun the process of the Islamization of Pakistani laws. Since Islam, like any faith, has multiple interpretations and jurisprudences, General Zia and his religious advisers had to choose an official version for themselves. There were multiple factors that influenced this choice including his proclivities towards the Jamaat-i-Islami leadership of the time and a close relationship with Saudi Arabia that he was nurturing.

The Jamaat-i-Islami, as a part of the martial law government in its initial years, was able to push its own thinking and ideology. Besides, General Zia felt very close to Mian Tufail Mohammad, the then leader of the Jamaat, in terms of both a shared clan and his view of the world. Additionally, due to a certain type of politics being promoted in the whole region by the Americans and the Saudis, the official faith of the Kingdom of Saudi Arabia could not simply be ignored, either by General Zia's military government or his preferred clerics. Therefore, the laws were Islamized according to a neo-purist view of Islam that spun-off the Sunni interpretation of the faith. This neo-purist view was an amalgam of Salafi (or, more accurately, neo-Salafi) principles, the Deobandi school of thought, and the views of Maulana Maududi, the founder of the Jamaat-i-Islami. Interestingly, even these schools had major differences until that time but the desire for power and domination can make bedfellows out of strangers. The Constitution of the Islamic Republic of Pakistan, in abeyance since General Zia took over, was amended in a certain ideological way when it was partially restored during that bout of martial rule.

The version of Islam promoted during General Zia ul-Haq's time was not followed or understood by the majority of Sunni Muslims either. Things have changed since. However, if I look back, in a society whose practices were historically influenced by the views of Ahmad Raza Khan Barelvi, founder of the Barelvi school of thought within Sunni Islam in the Indian subcontinent, or by the Sufi saints and poets of South and Central Asia, the neo-puritanism and rigidity introduced in the name of rational faith were disturbing for most individuals. Even while disagreeing with the official version of faith they were forced to follow. They were neither theologically prepared nor politically organized to put up any resistance. Even to this day, we find that the Council of Islamic Ideology, a statutory body to vet laws in Pakistan ensuring that they are in agreement with the injunctions of Islam, is dominated by Deobandi and other neo-purist clerics. Shia Muslims, who are more equipped in terms of their theology, jurisprudence, and clerical organization, reacted to the injunctions imposed on them differently than Barelvi Sunnis.

Iran had witnessed a bloody revolution in 1979. The clerics sidelined all secular, socialist, and plural forces who were their allies during the uprising, and created a Shia theocratic state in the name of Islam. The success of the revolution in Iran inspired many Muslims belonging to different sects all over the world. For Shias particularly, their theological base was strengthened and revived. Until then, a large number of South Asian, Shia Muslims did not believe in following a supreme religious leader present among them but this was significantly changed by the Iranian revolution. Shias were more organized as a community and challenged General Zia's blanket Islamization, occasionally taking to the streets. The banking rules, the inheritance laws, the Islamiat syllabus, et al, were to be worked out differently for them. Pakistan does not define itself as a Sunni Islamic Republic legally or constitutionally as there are some inclusive provisions for Shia Islam and other sects in its law books and official procedures. However, it certainly became a sectarian society with Sunni Islam as the only mainstream version of the faith. Law books are important. They reflect where the state stands in its role as an arbiter and negotiator between its citizens and institutions; and whether it aims to stay neutral and side with the weak or take a position favouring a powerful interest group or particular sets of interests.

I recall scores of Shia medical doctors marked and killed in Karachi during the 1990s and the trend spread to other places like Lahore. Prominent Shia professionals in all walks of life are attacked all over the country. The target killing of ordinary Shias and the bombing of their processions continue. This cannot just be brushed aside as a proxy war between Saudi Arabia and Iran anymore or as a conspiracy by foreign operators on our soil. The blame can no longer be shifted to external actors by our defence strategists and political analysts.

We are fragmenting fast. There is an implosion happening. There are no widespread riots but the Shia-Sunni divide is at its worst in the history of Pakistan. It is not only the lunar Islamic month of Muharram when Shias bring out processions or hold meetings and special prayers that is sensitive; Shia Muslims are targeted all round the year. When the pulpit is instilling hate in the hearts and minds of people, it is important for Pakistanis who believe otherwise to raise their voice. They have to speak up, else the silence will haunt their future generations. Although the founder of Pakistan did not believe in any form of sectarian association, it is historically correct that he was born into a Shia and Ismaili family. His wedding with Ruttie Bai, a Zoroastrian woman whom he courted, was performed according to the Shia Muslim way. His sister, one of the icons of Pakistan's struggle for democracy, Fatima Jinnah, held a Majlis-i-Aza to mourn his death in 1948. This is a ritual observed only by Shias after someone's passing away. You remember the sacrifice of Husain, the grandson of the Prophet of Islam and his family in Karbala, present day Iraq, about 1,400 years ago. Husain challenged monarchy and refused to pledge allegiance to an unjust ruler. Given the existence of these practices in Jinnah's family, it is quite ironic to now witness the purging of Shia Muslims in Pakistan. Allama Iqbal wrote verses in praise of Ali Ibn Abi Talib, the first Imam and the fourth Caliph of Muslims, in both Persian and Urdu, and said he considered Ali his true and only spiritual leader. Iqbal was born to a Sunni family. Three out of four major Sufi traditions in Islam identify Ali as their spiritual leader.

Just as a significant number of Pakistanis disowned Dr Abdus Salam, the first Nobel laureate the country produced, for his Ahmadi faith, I hope that the time will never come when Shia scientists, professionals, artists, and writers are also repudiated. How barren Pakistan and its society will become if the contribution of non-Sunnis to the collective civilization, culture, thinking, and sensibility is discounted. If individuals who may not have been the followers of

Shia jurisprudence, but believe in the greatness of Ali as the beacon of knowledge, wisdom, and spirituality are added to the list, few will be left for a mention in our intellectual and cultural history. It is also complicated because, even today, Shias and Sunnis cannot be clearly differentiated in many communities. Like their fundamental beliefs, their families are also intertwined. As boys in our early teens, to recall from personal memory, the first time we came to know about who was Shia or Sunni from within our Muslim classmates was when we were made to choose the Islamiat textbook. Rather than bringing Muslims together, General Zia ul-Haq's Islamization fractured them.

There were so many of us who came from multi-sectarian and multi-ethnic families. Even those who did not come from such mixed backgrounds respected the differences. We were systematically divided. Many Sunnis on the paternal side of my family believed in the reverence, pre-eminence, and superiority of Ali in knowledge and wisdom and were called *Tafzili*. However, my father's uncle was *Ahle Hadith*, the farthest from Shia beliefs and practices one could get in the Indian subcontinent of the nineteenth and early twentieth centuries. In the 1940s, he arranged his son's marriage to a second cousin's daughter who was Shia. Perhaps that was not commonplace but not impossible either. In 2013, when a twenty-six-year-old cousin of mine, Sobhan Warsi, was murdered on the first day of Muharram, the police in Karachi found it hard to believe that the uncle of a boy born to a Shia mother was Sunni. It took his uncle some time to convince the hospital and police authorities to recover his nephew's body for burial. While preparing for the upcoming processions, my cousin was taking a horse from one place to another when he was twice shot in the head. The horse was shot eight times. A horse is used to symbolize the horse of Husain during the Muharram processions.

Barelvi Sunnis and their political organizations like Sunni Tehrik or JUP have also become more militant to secure their turf. They are not anti-Shia but their recent mobilization in favour of General Zia ul-Haq's blasphemy law is a major example of the desire to reclaim the territory they seem to have lost to more militant outfits belonging to other schools of thought. However, they are seen as adulterators in 'real' Islam by the more extreme amongst the orthodox Sunni sub-sects and especially by the neo-purists. Something alarming that began happening in recent years is the preparation of another battle amongst Sunnis themselves, between *Muqallid* and *Ghair-Muqallid* schools: one literalist and the other symbolist.

The persecution of Shias in Pakistan today is an indicator of the increase in magnitude of religious extremism in the country. The persecution is not carried out by the state. However, it is certainly due to the long-held policies of the state that led society to discriminate against them on a wide scale. In old tribal societies, when a murder had to be avenged and there was no man in the family who could be killed, the avengers waited for years till the boys in that family grew up. Today, the killers have no such patience.

Shia Muslims in most parts of Pakistan, in theory, can give different and more universal names to their new born babies or rename the older ones to be saved from instant persecution. But what do the Hazara Shias of Balochistan do? How many of them can have their facial features surgically changed? Hazaras are killed in large numbers with impunity. They are attacked in their mosques, in bazaars, in neighbourhoods, and dismounted from buses and killed. I had known Irfan Ali Khudi, the thirty-two-year-old human rights defender, a gentle, serene soul, since he had moved to Islamabad. He was visiting Quetta to meet his family when, on that fateful day, there were two bomb blasts in their colony. After the first blast, the moans and cries of the maimed and the wounded made people nearby run towards the site of the attack to rescue the survivors. Then came the second blast killing or injuring those who had rushed to rescue the victims of the first explosion. Irfan was killed. Saeeda Bibi survives to witness death and destruction from close quarters. She had given birth to an amazing boy and, after losing her husband at an early age, reared her son to become what he was.

****

Not exactly like Hazaras but another group of people in Pakistan who are rather easily identified and categorized are the poor, minority Christians in the province of Punjab. They are settled in other provinces as well. Aasiya Noreen, more well-known as Aasiya Bibi, is one of the victims of the misuse of the blasphemy law, a law in Pakistan and other former British colonies that was there on the books but was heavily amended in the 1980s under General Zia ul-Haq. More than that, she is a victim of her circumstances—being poor, a woman, and a non-Muslim. Although the majority of the victims of the blasphemy law are Muslims, the minority Christians in the province of Punjab are the worst sufferers. One reason being their social class. Aasiya Bibi was accused of blasphemy near the town of Sheikhupura in central Punjab by co-workers. At the time I write this, her death sentence, awarded by a lower court in 2010 and upheld by Lahore High Court after five years, has been overturned by the Supreme Court of Pakistan, but this mother of five young children has been incarcerated for more than six years. In this arduous journey of fighting for justice, Salmaan Taseer, the governor of Punjab, and Shahbaz Bhatti, himself a Christian and a federal minister, lost their lives. Taseer was killed by his own security detail, Mumtaz Qadri. He had pumped twenty-seven bullets into Taseer's body and was caught, charged, sentenced, and executed. He confessed he was killing someone who had blasphemed and it was his religious duty to kill the blasphemer, an accusation which holds no ground by any standards, factual or legal. Another great campaigner for human rights, a friend and lawyer from Multan, Rashid Rehman, was shot in his chamber because he was representing a university lecturer accused of blasphemy, who happens to be a Muslim. He was also the nephew of our eminent public intellectual, seasoned journalist, and arch human rights defender, I. A. Rehman.

Christians in Punjab who are peasants, brick kiln workers, menial labourers, or small vendors have got the worst deal. Their churches are bombed, lands are encroached upon, houses and colonies are set on fire, and, furthermore, a young couple was thrown and burnt alive in an industrial furnace. For a moment, if we do not speak about more significant incidents of violence, rampage, assaults, arson, immolation, loot and plunder, forced marriages, and forced conversion that make the news and receive condemnation, let us just remind ourselves of how people treat them on a daily basis.

In the small towns of Punjab, Christian boys and girls are sometimes asked in school, not just by fellow students but teachers, why they do not convert if they are Pakistani. Also, their schoolmates ask them if their families celebrate 14 August as Independence Day. Zeeshan Noel, a committed community development activist and human rights campaigner, who comes from Rahim Yar Khan, a town in southern Punjab, once said that, while travelling on an intercity bus from Islamabad to his native town to celebrate Christmas or Easter with his parents, he conceals his identity. He never tells the person sitting next to him why he is going home. He says he is uncertain and afraid of the reaction of the fellow passengers upon knowing that he is Christian. Even if someone were to simply rob him of his possessions and then tell others that this Christian man has committed blasphemy, he would be lynched then and there.

Some years ago, another old colleague of mine, while travelling on a bus from one secondary town in central Punjab to another, was refused tea at a café and was asked to bring his own cup. They came to know he was not a Muslim because, when someone asked if he would be joining them for Friday prayers, he instinctively said that he was a Christian. Those who refused him a cup of tea were vendors who may have never seen a school and had little knowledge of religion but they were told by the clerics and members of the sectarian and religious militias operating in their villages and towns that non-Muslims cannot be served food and drinks in the same utensils as Muslims.

Numerous incidents of discrimination are perpetrated, consciously and unconsciously, in professional work environments and middle-class households, and not just in traditional feudal establishments. Ayub Malik, who retired as a naval officer but now works with a progressive political party, related an incident from his days of service. He received a complaint from a Christian staff member that a Muslim colleague had suddenly stopped eating with him and insisted that he keep a separate set of crockery and cutlery for himself. Malik summoned that Muslim staff member and inquired if he would ask a superior non-Muslim officer to do the same? He, of course, knew very well that this Muslim staff member worked under a non-Muslim Pakistani naval officer, washed his dishes, and polished his boots. There is a class element that gets introduced when we treat poor Christians and Hindus with contempt in Pakistan. In affluent households, where utensils for Christian servants are even further separated from those of Muslim servants, an ordinary, semi-literate European or American guest visiting Pakistan would be allowed to come and eat in Grandma's traditional china and porcelain.

Dhurmat was surprised when he was served food in a china plate. He was a janitor at a school in Karachi where my mother taught for more than thirty years. Supporting a family was tough on a meagre salary and, like everyone else in his profession, he would also work on his own in the evenings and during weekends for extra money. Everyone called him Dhurmat although that was not his real name. My mother had told me that his real name was Gurmukh (the face of the Guru) but it had become Dhurmat. I once asked him why. Dhurmat said that, when he turned eighteen and got this job in the school after an interview with the Administrator, he was introduced to the Principal. She misheard his name. She called him Dhurmat instead of Gurmukh and congratulated him for getting the job. She also told him that he was expected to work hard, something he never forgot. He would nod in agreement to anything she said without lifting his head. Then she introduced him to other staff and students in the morning assembly the next day calling him Dhurmat. He said that the Principal could never be wrong and he thought for many years that his illiterate father must have mispronounced his name and that it was, in fact, Dhurmat and not Gurmukh!

During recess at school, Dhurmat would get tired after scrubbing floors in the morning and cleaning bathrooms all day. Therefore, he was given something to eat by the teachers, a samosa or two, or a patty with a cup of tea. A number of times, I saw him squatting on the floor in a corner and facing the wall when eating. I asked him why he did that. He laughed at me and said I was young and did not understand that he was a low caste Hindu who cleaned toilets and mopped floors. Not just that, the other support staff members did not eat with him and did not want to see him eating in front of them. Dhurmat said that he was ten-years old when he lived near Ramaswami, an old neighbourhood in Karachi. A group of boys kicked him hard in his ribs when he drank water from the same hand pump they used to drink water from. Sometime after losing his eyesight due to consuming foul liquor, Dhurmat passed away. His son was employed in his place by the school.

Like Dhurmat, Yaqub Masih also died a natural death. He was neither killed in the Peshawar Church bombing nor lynched by a mob after being accused of blasphemy. He died of pneumonia and pleurisy in a Rawalpindi government hospital in 2013 leaving behind a widow, three sons, and two daughters. Since he was eight years old, he had worked as a janitor and sweeper, at various places, for fifty years. Two of his three sons remain janitors while one was lucky and able to get an entry level job with a contractor working for the government municipal service.

His widow, like any malnourished mother having gone through seven pregnancies (five survived, one was a still birth, and one child died of jaundice when six days old), has arthritis, brittle bones, and a perpetual backache ever since she entered her forties. She gave birth to the youngest son in that state. The two girls wash and clean in a middle-income neighbourhood just across the road from where Yaqub Masih's family live. The older one is engaged to be married into a family that lives in a village outside the city of Sialkot. The mother keeps delaying the marriage due to the expenditure it involves. Yaqub died after coughing every night for two years. Six working people, including his sons and daughters, could not afford decent treatment for him. His older son told me that the combined income of all five siblings, after Yaqub's death, is very small and, in that meagre amount, six people have to be fed, the rent for a two-room house in a squatter settlement has to be paid, and electricity and water bills have to be managed. Saving money for the sister's marriage is next to impossible.

Aasiya Bibi languishes in jail while optimistic human rights defenders, her five children, husband, relatives, and friends wait for something miraculous to happen. Even if she is released, ten-million Pakistanis or more like her will continue to live with a millstone cast in a furnace of poverty and a minority faith locked around their necks. In his essay 'The Necessity to Speak', Sam Hamill begins with a quote from Albert Camus stating that one must understand what fear means, what it implies, and what it rejects. It implies and rejects the same fact, a world where murder is legitimate and where human life is considered trifling. He says that, in the midst of a murderous world, we [should first] agree to reflect on murder and to make a choice. After that, we can distinguish between those who accept the consequences of being murderers themselves or the accomplices of murderers and those who refuse to do so with all their force and being. Since this terrible dividing line does actually exist, it will be a gain if it is clearly marked. Camus ends here but our work for those living in fear in Pakistan begins, be it the fear of being different, or the fear of being dispossessed.

****

There are people in Pakistan who clearly mark the dividing line and choose their side. One such person was Perween Rahman. I was terribly sad, but not surprised, when she was shot and killed. This is how we have been honouring the brave and the brilliant for some time. This is the recompense we give to those who decide to apply their education and training to serve the disadvantaged rather than earning dividends only for themselves hoping to join the affluent and the elite. There are physical, emotional, social, and economic costs a person coming from the educated and affluent middle class has to bear when deciding to side with and work for the weaker segments of society.

The conventional path for the social class Rahman belonged to is to climb the ladder of good fortune at a fast pace, aspire to be more rich and powerful, and continue to aid the elite by working for them or becoming a part of them by perpetuating their grip over state and society. Becoming one of the elite is the ultimate middle-class dream. There is a cost of speaking for the poor and writing for the oppressed in the face of an omnipotent system where elites and mafias collude to eliminate any difference, leave alone any challenge to their absolute authority. There is a bigger cost involved if you practically work for the well-being of the poor and oppressed. The cost is deadlier if you decide to work with the poor and oppressed to change their lives. When you work with them, hand in hand as equals, those who are kept weak for ages begin to find their own dignity and self-respect. This is lethal for the status quo. It cannot be permitted.

To me, Perween Rahman's work was not about housing for the poor teaching one how to lay down the sewerage system on one's own, in the squatter tenement in which one lives, providing credit to poor women for creating small and medium profitable enterprises, running schools for disadvantaged children, and setting up dispensaries for those who have no access to decent health facilities. These are ways, and undoubtedly significant ways, to transform how people live. Essentially, her work was about how people thought, most importantly about themselves, about their past, present, and future, what betterment they desired, and the changes they wanted in making the lives of their coming generations more respectable. Rahman's work was entirely about bringing dignity and self-respect to those who were treated like dirt by the rich and the powerful. Her work was about claiming a decent physical space for the working class of Karachi.

Rahman went beyond the rhetoric of change. She worked with people in practical terms, day in and day out, for bringing about the change in their lives and thinking. The Orangi Pilot Project (OPP), the institution Perween worked at for about thirty years, was founded by none other than Dr Akhtar Hameed Khan. Some social scientists may have theoretical and academic differences with what Dr Khan preached and practised but no one could ever doubt his integrity, uncompromising dedication, and unwavering commitment to empower common people through community action. He lived like a dervish and left a legacy in the shape of the OPP, the Urban Resource Centre, the rural support programmes intellectually led by Dr Shoaib Sultan Khan and scores of community organizations following his teachings in social and economic development across the length and breadth of Pakistan. He had earlier founded the Comilla Rural Academy in what is now Bangladesh and what later became the Bangladesh Academy for Rural Development.

Rahman was a true disciple of Dr Akhtar Hameed Khan in every possible sense. She lived like a dervish. There was a halo of innocence around her. Her sobriety, polished manners, reticent smile, and an unmatched dedication to her work made her shine. She was based in Karachi and spent most of the time working there but she helped activists from all over Pakistan and abroad to take Khan's philosophy and practice forward. In 1991, Arif Hasan introduced me to Rahman. Hasan is an extraordinary architect, planner, author, and teacher who oriented so many of us on how to understand the wide range of cultural, developmental, and political issues faced by the people of

Pakistan. In his cosy study, there were long evenings where friends
and students would sit and talk. From national politics to informal
economy, the plight of common folk and the remedies for setting
the course right, from anthropology and history to art and literature,
everything was under discussion. Perween Rahman was sometimes
present. She would listen to everyone patiently, make a remark once
in a while, smile when teased by a friend, and nod with candour when
she agreed with the point of view of someone who she would not agree
with on anything otherwise.

Karachi, the city Rahman lived and worked in, has been at the
mercy of killers and plunderers for a long time. It is one of the deadliest
cities in the world. From intellectual-philanthropist, Hakim Saeed, to
poet Raees Amrohvi; from journalist, Wali Khan Babar, and all the
six witnesses to his murder, to activist Nisar Baloch; from a sitting
provincial assembly member, Raza Haider, to a serving naval officer
Lt. Cdr. Azeem Haider, thousands have perished over the last three
decades. Hundreds of police personnel have lost their lives. Carjacking,
robberies, thefts, heists, mugging, and snatching, are all rampant.
There may be smaller reasons contributing but what turned Karachi
into killing fields are two major factors: a deep crisis of identity among
Muhajirs, people who themselves, or their ancestors, had migrated
from what is now India at the time of Partition, and a perpetual
conflict to control resources in general, and land in particular. Karachi
is the largest and the richest city in Pakistan, the jugular vein of the
country's economy, its principal seaport, main airport, industrial hub,
and financial centre.

I shall now delve into the emergence of the Muhajir identity
in Karachi and other parts of urban Sindh. How ironic that the
descendants of those South Asian Muslims who championed the
cause of creating a country on the basis of the Two Nation Theory,
Muslims and Hindus are two separate nations, now insist on having a
separate ethno-linguistic identity with some of them even demanding
a dedicated piece of land in Pakistan to be declared as their province.

The identity they claim to have today does not emanate from any primary characteristics determined by physical, racial, or geographic factors. Immigrants came to the province of Sindh from what are now fifteen or more different states in present day India, speaking different languages or dialects. Their bond is based on a shared sense of grievances whipped up by their political leadership, even much before the Muhajir Qaumi Movement (MQM)—later renamed the Muttahida Qaumi Movement—was formed, the party that, since 1987, is considered their representative voice. It remains the only example of its kind in Pakistan and perhaps the whole of the subcontinent where the third generation of immigrants would want a province of their own on the basis of an identity that is termed 'ethnic' by some but was non-existent sixty-years ago. It is indeed a reflection of Pakistan's unsettled political issues. Hindus and Sikhs migrated from what is now Pakistan to what is now India. They were called *sharnarthi* (refugee) in the initial years. But that remained a 'status' and did not turn into a demand for a separate 'ethnic' identity.

Karachi became the capital of Pakistan and, on Jinnah's insistence, was severed from Sindh. Muhajirs filled up many new federal government jobs and their elite rose to positions of power. Sindh had a very small Muslim middle class at the time of Partition in 1947. Muhajirs filled the vacuum created by the exodus of Hindus and constituted a majority in Karachi besides being dominant in some other cities of Sindh. The Muhajir elite shared absolute power with the Punjabis in the government and bureaucracy of Pakistan. The Muhajir middle class was absorbed in the newly emerging media and professional services. A sizeable number of upper and middle class Muhajirs filed claims, bogus or real, to possess properties left by Hindus and Sikhs in lieu of what they had left in India. A large number of Muhajirs lived in harsh conditions but they had a much larger affluent middle class than the local population. With Punjabis, Muhajirs were the main proponents of Pakistani nationalism on the basis of the Two Nation Theory and supported a strong centre, denying the existence of a heterogeneous state and people around them.

In 1958, martial law was imposed by General Ayub Khan. The rise of a military in which Punjabis constituted the largest part, followed by Pakhtuns and Hindko-speaking Hazara-wals from Pakhtunkhwa (it is just the region they belong to that is called Hazara, but the people have little in common with the Hazaras of Balochistan), meant a decrease in the powers of civilian bureaucracy largely dominated by Muhajirs. On top of it, the General decided to shift the capital to a purpose-built city falling between Rawalpindi (where the army was headquartered), and Haripur, the place he hailed from. This was a clear message to Muhajirs that, from now on, they would have a secondary role in running the affairs of the state.

The Muslim League increasingly became a party of Punjabis during that period with a part of the leadership aligning itself with army rule. A large number of Muhajirs turned towards Islamist parties like the Jamaat-i-Islami and the Jamiat-e-Ulema-i-Pakistan. Islamist parties were against the military rule of General Ayub due to its somewhat secular nature and professed Pakistan's nationhood on the basis of Islam. However, the participation of a segment of Muhajirs in the pro-democracy campaigns and their significant contribution to the progressive student and labour movements cannot be ignored.

Karachi received a large number of Bihari refugees from former East Pakistan after the bloodbath of 1971. Their contention was that Pakistan was created as a homeland for South Asian Muslims and not a country to be based on Bengali nationalism. This made them side with the West Pakistan-dominated army and suffer hugely at the hands of Mukti Bahini and other Bengali militant groups. They had no choice but to leave and Karachi was their destination. More than two-hundred and fifty thousand were left behind to languish in refugee camps and could never be repatriated to Pakistan due to its internal political problems and ethnic tensions. After 1971, the PPP government continued the policy of a strong centre with

Bhutto's political choices and use of force causing unrest in the North West Frontier Province (NWFP), now Khyber Pakhtunkhwa, and Balochistan. However, on the socio-cultural plane, the government, media, and school syllabus started acknowledging different ethno-linguistic groups in Pakistan.

In order to provide educational and employment opportunities to the long-deprived rural Sindhi population, a quota system was introduced on the urban-rural basis in the 1970s. This meant a further reduction in government jobs for Muhajirs. Karachi, where more than half of the Muhajir population was settled, had remained separated from Sindh from 1948 to 1970. It now became the capital of Sindh. Sindhi was declared the official language in the province along with Urdu. Sindhi-Muhajir riots broke out in the province. The twenty-two year administrative divide of Sindh had led to a political schism for decades to come. During General Zia ul-Haq's martial rule in Pakistan (1977–88), the internal migration from Khyber Pakhtunkhwa and Punjab to Karachi rose to new levels. The quota system to ensure rural Sindh's participation in jobs was further extended. Afghan refugees also started pouring in. All of this resulted in a further shrinking of opportunities and space for Muhajirs.

In the early 1980s, the Movement for the Restoration of Democracy (MRD) began and Sindh became its main battleground. Muhajir-dominated cities remained calm. Although G. M. Syed, the founder of Sindhi-nationalist Jeay Sindh Mahaz (JSM) that had supported secession from Pakistan for a while, also chose not to support the MRD, it was Muhajir docility that grieved the Sindhis more because it was not the JSM but the PPP that was their representative party. When the autocratic MQM leader, Altaf Hussain, first appeared on the political map, he was welcomed and garlanded in the JSM headquarters by their leadership.

When General Zia ul-Haq repressed political forces that enjoyed country-wide presence, particularly the PPP, and encouraged regionalization of politics, Muhajirs, a community of people stigmatized by the logic of domination and in search of a source of meaning, concreted a political identity, claiming that it was an ethno-linguistic identity. The demand for Muhajir recognition as a fifth nationality, the other four being Punjabi, Sindhi, Pathan, and Baloch, gained momentum during the 1980s. Since the 1970s, Pakistani school curricula and the state-run media had started showing four distinct images of people, on the basis of four provinces, to depict diversity in Pakistan. Seraiki or other linguistic and national rights movements had not gained as much currency as they did later. Since Pakistan was run as a unitary state rather than a real federation, the resistance to centralized state policies was expressed in terms of ethno-nationalism. A segment of Muhajir political leadership decided to take the same course after first being relegated to junior partners to Punjabis in running the affairs of the state and then being further sidelined with people from other regions claiming their right to state power and privileges. As a result, the cities of Karachi and Hyderabad in Sindh witnessed massive rioting, violence, and military-led clean-up operations leading to the MQM hardening its control over urban Sindh. Altaf Hussain was ruthless in dealing with adversaries and dissent within the party ranks.

After their main political party has been in power multiple times for long years, be it through coalition with civilian political parties or under the martial law of General Pervez Musharraf, exercising formidable control over many Sindhi resources, having the longest-serving governor of the province ever and participating in decision making at the provincial and federal levels through a sizeable representation in Parliament and the assemblies, there is little reason or cause for Muhajirs to ask for a separate province on an ethno-linguistic basis. Nonetheless, the MQM has native-ized the Muhajir population completely into a local identity that asserts itself within the polity of Pakistan. However, Muhajirs can only be Pakistanis, unlike Pakhtuns, Punjabis, and others, as their very identity is linked to the migration of population from what is now India to what is now Pakistan.

There is a war over resources and land between political organizations and mafias organized on ethnic and religious bases. As a consequence of permanent unrest in many parts of Karachi, there is a complete breakdown of municipal services. Pakistan's federal government and military-run enterprises are major stakeholders in the riches Karachi has to offer. I lost another friend to the land mafia who was also a comrade-in-arms with Perween Rahman but worked in a different area. Nisar Hussain Baloch was a housing rights defender, a community rights campaigner, a voice of the poor, and a beacon of hope for the downtrodden Baloch and Sindhi population of the old parts of the great metropolis. These are people who have inhabited Karachi since it was a fishing village in the eighteenth century. Baloch left a widow, a toddler, and hundreds of thousands of victims of illegal land encroachment behind him to grieve his murder and mourn their fate.

Nisar Baloch was critical of both, the coercion and intolerance faced by activists like him at the hands of the MQM on the one hand, and the expediency and tardiness of the PPP government in that period. He became the President of the 'Gutter Bagheecha Bachao Tehrik' (Save the Gutter Park Movement), and worked closely with organizations like Shehri and other citizens rights groups to marshal public support for his cause. Already, out of 1,017 acres, four-hundred and eighty acres were left as the amenity park and the women and children of the area used it for leisure and respite from the heavily industrialized and polluted environs of the old city. In 2009, the night when Nisar Baloch returned from the Civil Hospital, Karachi, after attending to the wounded men and women attacked while peacefully protesting against encroachment in the name of building colonies and commercial enterprises, he was shot and killed. Some old areas of the city were shut down in protest and people raised slogans against the government. Baloch's passion was educating the young in his low-income neighbourhood. He started his career in social work by establishing a street school where children were taught free. Due to his political consciousness and a deep desire to change the world around him in favour of the disadvantaged, he soon became active in the areas of environmental conservation and the provision of basic facilities to those who have been kept at a sub-human level by powers that prevail. His consciousness cost him his life.

Gutter Bagheecha is just one example. The governments in Karachi, local and provincial, changed the status of at least twenty-six parks and playgrounds in middle, lower-middle, and working-class areas of the city. When a large tract of land by the sea was converted into a modern park on the outskirts of a rich neighbourhood, the underprivileged residents of the metropolis were denied their right to public spaces and amenity plots. This is a city where different forms of municipal administrative services have a history of no less than a century and a half, six cantonment boards, and other institutions possessing large tracts of land. Today, gutters are overflowing, solid waste is heaped along the pavements, streets are stinking, and the traffic on the roads and by-lanes is rough and undisciplined. None of the residential buildings are ever renovated or painted. Long and short cables and wires of electricity, telephone, and television connections enmesh the sky. Karachi is an arid area but it was never so bad as individuals and municipal administrations planted trees, tried to build parks, and create green patches wherever they could. Now, in poor neighbourhoods, there is not even a blade of grass to be seen. Occasionally, one can find the thorny keekar tree boasting its brownish green presence on the otherwise dry and dusty plains. Most Karachiites do not just live without potable water, proper sanitation, drainage, and without electricity and gas like the rest of the country. They, in fact, live in far more dangerous conditions than those in small towns and villages due to the unregulated and unsafe construction of buildings. The passes, underpasses, bypasses, overpasses, bridges, and ramps worth billions of rupees built by celebrated municipal governments and provincial administrations over the years, have not solved the issue of traffic congestion. The seminal work needed to understand Karachi, the issues faced by its inhabitants over the recent years, its sociology and literature, happens to be in Urdu. It is the special edition of two volumes published by *Aaj*, a worthy literary journal, edited by writer and critic Ajmal Kamal.

Gutter Bagheecha represents any public space in Pakistan for the poor. The neighbourhoods of Orangi and Baldia town where Rahman essentially worked can very well be the residential colonies for the poor anywhere. Karachi heralds urbanization and therefore reflects the urban planning, or the lack thereof, in the whole country. The land, transport, and water supply mafias, in cahoots with large business interests, control the city of Karachi. They are increasingly controlling every city in Pakistan and eliminating the Perween Rahmans one by one. It is not important whether the terrorist or the mercenary who pulled the trigger was identified or not, nor whether he was killed soon after in a police encounter or not. Someone was seriously motivated to have her killed. It could be someone belonging to the land grabbing mafia that she challenged through her work as she struggled alongside the disadvantaged for access to fundamental municipal services and better economic opportunities. Or, it could be a bigot who found the existence of an independent woman in his neighbourhood threatening to his ideology and values as she was influencing other women and men to come out of the traps of poverty and ignorance.

****

Sabeen Mahmud was much younger than Perween Rahman. The last time I met her was at the Beach Luxury Hotel in Karachi during the 2015 edition of a literary festival. She and our mutual friend, Zaheer Kidvai, invited me to visit The Second Floor (T2F) and read poetry when in Karachi next. Mahmud was to be gunned down two months after extending that invite.

T2F was a cultural space managed by Sabeen Mahmud for some years. It has a café, a small bookstore, a mini Hyde Park corner for airing dissent, and an open space for the performing arts, all rolled into one. The most appropriate description of her appeared in the weekly *Economist* in her obituary. It said that, in the midst of an anarchic, dysfunctional, crammed, crazy, noisy Karachi, was a woman who was even more anarchic, crazy, noisy, and in-your-face. She was at the heart of every disturbance; from supporting rank outsiders in local elections to organizing flash protests on social media, she spiced up every organization she belonged to which was any outfit committed to challenging discrimination or injustice.

As in the case of Perween Rahman's murder, it was announced by the authorities, some weeks later, that the killers of Sabeen Mahmud had been found. These young men who espoused extremist religious ideology, that had attacked a bus of Ismaili Muslims killing seventeen women and men in 2015, also confessed to killing her. The artists, poets, writers, and activists in Karachi and elsewhere in Pakistan do not know what to believe. A few days before her death, she was also asked not to organize a talk based on the disappearances of political workers and clean-up operations against secessionists in Balochistan.

Who would disagree that, in addition to defending the borders and ensuring its territorial integrity, any state in the world will act to curb insurgency and separatism within its borders? Irrespective of whether that state is run like a federation or a unitary entity. In the world of today, where monarchic empires no longer exist, a modern nation-state has to be subservient to the will of its citizens without discriminating among them. The state either has to be fully neutral or else has to demonstrate an inclination in favour of its weak and dispossessed citizens, Baloch, in this instance. This work is always a long haul and needs enormous amounts of patience.

Pakistan works as a federation but the size of its biggest province, Punjab, in terms of population, makes it a lop-sided federation. All major decisions are made on the basis of population, the count of which remains inaccurate, but we all know the general demographics tend to favour the largest province. Punjab has its own share of poverty and destitution but it does remain the most developed province in terms of social and economic indicators. By virtue of getting sustained, rather ever-increasing opportunities for better education and skill development are fostered in Punjab and, therefore, people from areas with better facilities dominate the emerging private sector. Constitutionally, Pakistan is a federation with a bicameral parliamentary system of governance. Most powers are vested in the lower house, the National Assembly, which is directly elected on the basis of constituencies demarcated according to the size of the population. Therefore, one province clearly dominates the federation. This is seen as pure democratic logic. However, the success of democracy does not only lie in a clear-cut rule of the majority, but in equally and fully accommodating minorities, ethnic, religious, or otherwise, in the process of governance and decision-making.

Further to its under-representation in every possible sphere, the Pakistani state has seen Balochistan, not through the eyes of its people but, as a part of its territory. We must not forget that, until some years ago, when we were cooking *chapattis* in Karachi and Lahore, on stoves fuelled by piped natural gas from Sui in Balochistan, residents in Balochistan had no gas connections at all, not even to heat their living rooms during the harsh winters. The apologists of the Pakistani state argue that it is the tribal chieftains of the Baloch who do not want any progress or development. As if the pockets of development in Sindh and Punjab were made possible by the efforts of the local landlords, influential traders, and businessmen in these areas. It is the responsibility of the state to ensure equal rights and provide similar services to all of its citizens. If traditional power structures exist in the country, it is the state that should have weakened those by taking progressive developmental actions. The same is true for other underdeveloped and deprived parts of the country, including the Federally Administered Tribal Areas (FATA).

The crisis in Balochistan has a history of disrespect, mismanagement, highhandedness, and injustice demonstrated by the leaders of the country. The forced annexation of the native state of Kalat, after the creation of Pakistan, instead of a peaceful, democratic process of annexation through negotiation was something Jinnah and the political cabal surrounding him should have avoided. Instead of using the pretext of the local nawabs from Kharan and Makran (regional rulers within the Kalat state), inviting the Pakistan government to intervene, a more civil path should have been chosen. The forced annexation did not sit well with many Baloch political workers and intellectuals of that time. However, the real trouble began when the Pakistani establishment, under General Ayub Khan, started dealing with the Baloch leadership with utter contempt. The worst example is the breaking of an oath with Sardar Nauroz Khan, the chief of the Zehri tribe. During the armed struggle of 1960, to resist the One-Unit administrative setup in West Pakistan, meaning the dissolution of West Pakistan's four federating units into one administrative zone bringing political parity with the then East Pakistan, Ayub's junta swore an oath and urged Nauroz Khan to surrender and prepare for negotiations. Nauroz Khan was betrayed and arrested. His sons were hanged in Hyderabad and Sukkur jails in Sindh. He died soon after in 1962.

Prime Minister Zulfikar Ali Bhutto, who was hanged in 1979, and his successors, General Zia ul-Haq and General Pervez Musharraf, were no different from General Ayub Khan when it came to making an attempt to understand, let alone respect, the rights of the Baloch people. Ironically, another major tribal chieftain from Balochistan, Nawab Akbar Bugti, worked closely with the Pakistani establishment just a few years before turning against it. The state could not keep him happy either, someone who had served as the Governor of the province and a Federal Minister of State for Interior Affairs, a highly sensitive public office.

The truth is not very simple in the case of Baloch tribal leaders impeding development in Balochistan. After Nauroz Khan's death in 1962, Baloch leaders sat together and prepared a document to negotiate with General Ayub. It was drafted by Sardar Sherbaz Mazari who is a Baloch but did not live in Balochistan. Maulana Bhashani, the veteran Leftist politician from East Pakistan, was requested to represent the Baloch leadership and meet the General. The Baloch asked for the release of prisoners and restoration of their property as the property of declared 'traitors' had been confiscated by the Ayub regime. They demanded a university in the province as there was none at that time. They wanted the government to make school education compulsory and free, construct a college in each district, a high school in each *tehsil* (sub-district), a primary school in each village, a dispensary in a sizeable village, and a hospital in each *tehsil*. They called for the construction of roads in the province and the development of harbours and fisheries on Balochistan's coast. They demanded that public servants of lower grades must be permanent residents of Balochistan and local labour should be recruited on developmental projects. Their demands prove that the Baloch leadership was not against the development of their own people.

Today, there may well be foreign involvement in Balochistan as the government says. However, the foreigners can only train and arm the insurgents. Who produces them? What is the point in asking universities, think-tanks, non-profit organizations, or cultural spaces like those run by Sabeen Mahmud not to raise the issues faced by Balochistan? How will a conversation in Lahore University of Management Sciences, or T2F in Karachi, fan the fire of secession in Balochistan? It will have exactly the opposite effect when the angry political workers and intelligentsia of Balochistan find people in other parts of Pakistan showing solidarity with them.

Let me come to the claim the government has made: the killers of Mahmud have been nabbed and the reprimands she received from the security agencies had nothing whatsoever to do with her murder. Of course, there is no hard evidence available otherwise to prove that the government is wrong. However, it is incredibly ironic that the state thinks that if its own institutions are not directly involved in killing a citizen, the state's name is cleared and it stands absolved of any responsibility. The foremost responsibility of any state is to protect its citizens.

******

Terry Eagleton, a British literary theorist and intellectual, says that power, to be effective, must inscribe itself on the senses. Extremist militants in Pakistan know that well. They instil fear in the hearts and minds of people by terrorizing and killing in the name of Islam. They are armed to the teeth and continually perpetrate violence to further their aims. The policies pursued and strategies applied by the Pakistani state and its dominant civil and military institutions within and outside the country have created an intolerant society, parts of which provide legitimacy to any action in the name of faith, even if that action is coercive and violent in nature. Political parties using religion as their ideological platform and proselytizing groups like the Tableeghi Jamaat continue to create legitimacy for an exclusive form of faith in their own supposedly benign way. To me, it is not benign at all. Many Pakistanis who come under their influence from affluent or the not-so-affluent middle class, particularly those living in the diaspora, cannot put up with anything different from their world-view, anything that may differ from their own belief system, and anything that forces them to question and think. Facts are dismissed summarily if there is an iota of doubt that they may challenge preconceived thoughts and ideas about Pakistan and Islam. Military dictators get redeemed in such people's imagination some years after a martial law ends because, unless a caliphate with its capital in Pakistan is not established, the country will remain in a state of war. David Grossman says that it is highly rational for a nation always in a state of war to elect combatants as its leaders. The fact that combatants are the nation's leaders decrees that the nation remains in a constant state of war. An abstract pan-Islamism and the desire to establish God's caliphate on the planet, which is entirely rooted in an imagined past, hinders the development of an indigenous narrative for Pakistan. The only political instrument that can develop that indigenous narrative is democracy—more power to the people, more representation, more participation, and more inclusion.

Many middle-class Pakistanis, who find the strength to question the political role played by the military once that rule is over, single out the General who imposes martial rule and absolve his organization of any role played in that act of subverting the Constitution. They, however, reject outright the principles, systems, institutions, and structure of democracy as a whole when some elected political leader falls short of delivering on his promises.

In all fairness, it is not just the military that prevented democracy from taking root in Pakistan. Turn the clock back to 1947 and the initial years of the country after Independence. West Pakistan's political and administrative space was fully captured by the landed elite, mostly from Punjab and some from Sindh, working in collaboration with the immigrant Muslim elite largely from northern India who had come to Pakistan along with the officers of the colonialist Indian Civil Service. Their protégé was to become the Pakistani Civil Service—bureaucrats, most of whom were self-serving and power hungry from day one, who looked down upon the poor natives as irrational, pre-modern, and unfit to participate in political processes. The seeds of this power capture were sown a little before the partition of British India when the feudal-led Unionist Party of Punjab merged into the Muslim League. The new West Pakistani power elite, a combination of West Punjabi and Muhajir elites and intelligentsia, feared the largely non-feudal and politically aware majority living in the province of East Bengal that became East Pakistan.

Mian Iftikharuddin, the progressive politician from Punjab who had joined the All India Muslim League, gave an account of Quaid-i-Azam being humiliated at the hands of feudal lords like Daultana, Tiwana, and Gurmani when he tried to push for fresh land settlement, rehabilitation of agrarian communities from East Punjab, and agricultural reform. One of them categorically blamed Quaid-i-Azam for creating a problem in the shape of East Pakistan. It is important to note that people like Liaquat Ai Khan and Chaudhry Khaliquzzaman did not side with the Quaid in such matters. Because democracy in the newly-founded country would not only have meant a larger share in the political sphere for the people of East Pakistan, it would also have brought rather radical and pro-people political thinking into the mainstream politics of the predominantly feudal, tribal, and elitist western wing of the country.

Events that unfolded in the 1950s and 1960s give enough credence to the point being made. The West Pakistani elite did not let the Constitution be drawn up for nine long years until the principle of parity between East and West Pakistan was negotiated with political leaders from the larger population of the eastern province. Subsequently, the other reason linked to the first one that destabilized democracy was the political nurturing of military generals and senior officers in a primarily West Pakistani army by the same West Pakistani elite in order to stay in control of both East and West Pakistan. General Ayub Khan was taken into the cabinet as minister of defence as early as 1954. Politicians and bureaucrats were chiefly responsible for bringing the army into the political fold at that time.

Later, when Pakistan agreed to America's offer to become its ally in the Cold War against the Soviet Union and its allies, the army's Sandhurst and Dehradun graduates were patronized by the West and encouraged to the extent that they finally took over the government and became the rulers after abrogating the Constitution of 1956 just two years after its promulgation. The military rule that was established in 1958 has firmly entrenched the military into the body politic of the country over the years. The short civilian interludes, one after the break-up of the country from 1972 to 1977, then between 1988 and 1999, then again from 2008 until the present stand witness to the obvious political role played by the military. Initially, it was the West

Pakistani elite—and now it is their remnants, who can be called the civilian aiders, abettors, and collaborators (to borrow terms from the Constitution of 1973)—who contributed to martial rule. Neither has any martial rule strengthened the federation and served Pakistan's interests nor can they be expected to in the future. Not only must the military understand that, but, the self-serving politicians who can only make it to power if there is a non-representative government should as well.

The third and significant reason that undermined the democratic process is the role of the higher judiciary and legal community in condoning the sacking of governments and dissolution of successive parliaments beginning with Justice Munir's infamous Doctrine of Necessity and the acts of legal spin-doctors beginning from Sharifuddin Pirzada. These people proactively provided legal and constitutional cover to the political ambition of different rulers and dictators. It is now accepted by supporters of democracy and independent legal historians that, if Khwaja Nazimuddin's government, which was removed by Governor General Ghulam Mohammad, had been restored by Justice Munir's bench of the then Federal Court, Pakistan would have been a different country. Justices M. R. Kiyani, B. A. Siddiqui, Dorab Patel, Fakhruddin G. Ebrahim, Saeeduz Zaman Siddiqui, and a few others like them never budged on matters of principle but there were so many available to replace them. This seems to be changing now, but Pakistanis have to watch closely the recently found self-confidence of the superior judiciary and not become optimistic about their changing role. We may recall that many of the judges did take oath, just a few years ago, under the Provisional Constitutional Order and Judges Order when General Musharraf came to power in 1999. Some of these same judges, led by former Chief Justice Iftikhar Chaudhry, created a popular movement against General Musharraf after he sacked Chaudhry in 2007. However, they had actually taken oath under the General a few years earlier. Chaudhry was even a part of the bench that condoned General Musharraf's rule.

The final element that contributes to the weakening of democracy is the nature of the mainstream political parties. It is important to recognize that many of these parties operate in a restrictive political environment caused by military interference and irresponsible media reporting in recent times. However, now nothing stops their leadership from creating internally democratic and better organized parties with informed and knowledgeable cadres. As stated earlier, democracy is the only political instrument that can save Pakistan from the current high tide of extremism and violence but it will be a blunt instrument if political parties cannot live up to their promise as effective organizations of people.

It is so unfortunate that, at present, there is a political class in Pakistan that is sustaining the reactionary and conservative sentiment cultivated over the years in the country which is the bedrock for extremism and violence. From the religious parties of all hues and colours to the various factions of the Muslim League to the new fad that is the Pakistan Tehreek-i-Insaf (PTI), all are conformist neo-liberals when it comes to the national economy but continue to use the religious rhetoric in their politics. PTI's rank and file despises the very practice and institutions of politics while craving the most coveted political office for their leader, Imran Khan, at the same time. The political circumstances in Pakistan and the desire to find a messiah who will change our destiny overnight have made it possible for a grotesque mediocrity to play a hero's part, to borrow a phrase from Karl Marx.

But someone as intelligent as Zulfikar Ali Bhutto had fallen into this trap of political expediency of appeasing the clerics to perpetuate his political power much before the politicians of today. In 1974, Pakistan's parliament decided to declare Ahmadis non-Muslim. Even if the majority of other Muslim sects in Pakistan believe that Ahmadis are not Muslims, parliament was perhaps not the place to get a law regarding religious ex-communication enacted. In this case and in many others, Zulfikar Ali Bhutto and his government succumbed to the pressure of the extreme Right. Not only that, Ahmadis have increasingly faced violence and institutionalized discrimination since parliament's decision created more social space for prejudice toward other minority faiths and sects. After Bhutto, General Zia ul-Haq introduced or amended laws in the name of Islamization that still need a thorough review, even after certain new legislations, which happen to be meek, compromised attempts to neutralize the effect of these laws.

General Zia, his companions, and those who followed in his footsteps created or encouraged individuals and outfits preaching violent extremism and allowed them to operate in the cities, towns, villages, and settlements of Pakistan for some twisted strategic reasons. Without getting into the debate about what is right or wrong, just and unjust in world affairs, let us accept what the states and their intelligence operatives do if they want to neutralize or dominate another country. They recruit disgruntled people from the country they want to dominate. Pakistani institutions mobilized groups of men from within our own society to settle issues outside the country. The legitimacy to extremist individuals and groups was first provided by the Pakistani state's action and now it is being sustained by the state's lack of adequate concerted action if not complete inaction.

Conquered, saddened, defeated and left behind by other human societies in so many walks of life, with a putrefied present and a shaky future, the traditional champions of Pakistani ideology and establishment have their faces of patriotism pockmarked by boils and blisters of hypocrisy and pomposity. They are hypocritical when it comes to using religious symbolism to further their worldly power and economic interests, and pompous when relating stories of a glorious past. I am always amused when a middle-aged Pakistani corner shop owner in the UK, or a cab driver in the US who never found a decent job in his home country, is somehow overawed by the greatness of the past. After having a filling dinner of biryani, they tell me that the West actually owes all of its development to us Muslims and that we, in the middle-ages, were the torchbearers of all knowledge and science. I find the use of 'us' and 'we' interesting to say the least for I know the distance between medieval Baghdad and the Islamabad of today.

The reactionary religious preachers proclaim that matters of life are predetermined with every question having been answered in the past. The problem with the Leftist dogmatists in Pakistan is that they claim to be scientific and rational but, in practice, base their arguments on the axioms of their favoured theorists of the bygone era rather than applying any philosophical tools methodically and afresh. In Pakistan, these two ideological camps continuously refer to old analyses to scope doctrines in case of faith and manifestos in case of political theory.

In the previous essay, I wrote about a generation of idealists who had difficult lives. Some had to spend years in jail, some were exiled, some had borne torture under oppressive regimes, and some found it hard to make ends meet—all in the name of bringing a revolution but few were systematically assassinated. In my times, it is not just Benazir Bhutto who is murdered. My contemporaries who are not even revolutionaries but fighting for simple human causes are indiscriminately killed. Two such people from the literati and media, who were lucky to survive attempts made on their lives, are Asghar Nadeem Syed and Raza Rumi. However, Rumi's twenty-seven year old driver was killed in that attack in front of his eyes.

In Pakistan, we have seen so much death and destruction over the past twenty years that many of us feel exactly what Khet Mar, the Burmese writer who faced prison and exile, once wrote. She said, 'Each night when I lie down in my bed, an infernal sleep accompanied by a series of nightmares begins.'

4

Ink

The caged bird sings
— Maya Angelou

THERE WERE TWO FASCINATING TEACHERS OF ENGLISH LANGUAGE and literature at my school. The soft and skinny Sir Maya Das Nayyer, who taught us for five years between 1977 and 1982, and the hard and hefty Miss Catherine Val D'Eremao, who would teach our class when Sir Das was away on leave. In Pakistan my generation was in the habit of using the prefixes 'Sir', 'Madam', or 'Miss' for our teachers when addressing them or referring to them. After so many years I still cherish the moments when Miss Val as she was popularly known, gave us lessons on Wordsworth and Keats. She also believed that we were lagging behind the rest of the world because we did not give due importance to the English language. She was an old, Karachi native of Goan origin, English-speaking, and dusky-skinned. Her forbearers had settled in the city probably more than one-hundred and fifty years ago. She wore elegant sarees and walked slowly, with a slight bend towards the right, as if she had a limp in her leg. Sir Das was from a village outside Sialkot, a historic city in central Punjab, and occasionally wrote traditional forms of poetry in Urdu. He also played the harmonium and supervised the school's music society before it was disbanded by the administration after General Zia ul-Haq took over.

Sir Das was a teacher of English literature but attached equal importance to learning Urdu. However, according to Miss Val, using

English in all walks of life and enforcing it as the only lingua franca in the country was the panacea for all our intellectual shortcomings and social ills in Pakistan. Once, in class she said that those of her students whose parents know the language must speak English at home. I remember coming back from school and sharing her view with my father. Without even raising his eyes from the book he was reading, he said he was not sure if that was a good idea. I should learn as many languages as I can, but not at the cost of my own.

Perhaps, she was an ideational predecessor to some of our arch liberal thinkers of the Third World today who earnestly believe that adopting the English language is the only key to our becoming modern in thinking and a precondition to our intellectual liberation. They overlook the fact that the Chinese, Japanese, French, Germans, Scandinavians, and to an extent, Turks, could develop in all respects without English; and, at times, people of grossly limited intellect or a myopic view of the world get popularly elected as leaders in English-speaking countries.

Things have changed in Pakistan since the times of Miss Val. I would rather say they have been made to change: in a particular fashion to benefit particular people. When on the one hand, there is much hue and cry about teaching English to children and young people, on the other hand, the language divide is being widened across the state and society. Miss Val wanted every child to be schooled in English. In Pakistan, English is the language that brings power, prosperity, privilege, and prestige. It is not for everybody. The selective promotion of English, latent and overt, is not directed at culturally modernizing Pakistan and expediting its intellectual development, even if one agrees with that assertion. But it is there to ensure the exclusion of the majority of people from participating in making decisions that affect their lives. If that were not the case, all children going to school would be granted a similar education. How ironic that the affairs of the state are run in a language that is either not taught at all or not instructed properly to eighty per cent of our school-going children. A large percentage of that school-going age spend their time on the streets, on farms, in shops, or in factories anyway.

I was introduced to the story of a woman named Saima some years ago while working on a paper about education governance in Pakistan that also looked at issues of language and education. Saima went to school in the late 1980s and 1990s. She was born to the family of a struggling barber who would also work as a farmhand, during the harvesting season, in a village outside the semi-urban town of Gujjar Khan in the Rawalpindi district of northern Punjab. One of her legs was affected by polio. Growing up in a country where due to malnutrition, even the weak strains of inoculation cause the disease in some children in remote areas before they are anathematized for life— Saima was a little luckier than others. Supported by her classmates in the village, she would limp her way to school and she topped the finishing exam of the primary school. A charitable retired colonel from the army, who came from her village, was impressed by her exceptional feat. He helped her get admission into the best secondary school in the area, run by the municipal committee in Gujjar Khan. After finishing primary school from their nearby villages or from some school in Gujjar Khan, getting admission in this secondary school was considered quite competitive. The school always produced good results in middle and matriculation exams held under the Rawalpindi Board.

Saima started doing well in most subjects in the sixth grade. However, for many months, she was penalized, caned, and sent out of the class by a strict teacher. Her classmates felt bad, and the village barber never found the strength to speak to the teacher or the principal of the school when the girl told her parents what she was going through. She struggled and suffered in silence. Since she was bright and had put in extra effort to learn the subject, she passed her exam. But she continued to neglect other subjects as a consequence and never topped again. The subject that one of the brightest of our girls struggled with, in secondary school, was English Language: Comprehension and Composition. No one had ever spoken English around Saima in her village. She did not know what a comic book was and neither had she ever watched a cartoon in English. She was not familiar with 'Charlie's Chocolate Factory', and she had never heard about Robert Louis Stevenson and his railway carriage. The only place she had visited outside her village was Gujjar Khan. Only once had she attended a wedding ceremony in Rawalpindi with her family.

The gulf between the two linguistic worlds has widened so much over the years that less of my bucolic demeanour and more of my grounding in Urdu literature initially made some literary editors and critics think that I must have attended a local madrasah or a purely Urdu-medium school. Some time ago, I was asked by the editors of 'Books & Authors', the small magazine dedicated to literature and writing brought out with the Sunday edition of the Pakistani daily newspaper *Dawn*, to relate my experience writing and publishing in more than one language. I write in both Urdu and English with an occasional verse or two in Punjabi, and at times naturally throw in words and phrases from Persian, other Pakistani and North Indian languages in my Urdu verse. They were not the first ones to be intrigued by the possibility of someone using more than one language for creative expression. We still have people who are multilingual and write in both Urdu and English with equal felicity, but it is somehow becoming rare to find a person writing in both Urdu and English, particularly to produce creative literature. Curiously enough, bilingualism does not capture so much attention if one is writing in two vernaculars, such as Sindhi and Urdu, or Seraiki and Balochi. It becomes striking when English is the language in which you write other than your own. It is because the affluent urban, middle-class Pakistani is fast becoming monolingual and finds it really exotic that someone can write in English and a local vernacular at the same time.

Culturally, the people of Pakistan are also the successors of what one can call the Persio-Indo-Gangetic civilization. There is nothing unusual or rare about writing creatively in more than one language or using multiple dialects if we look at our intellectual and literary tradition. Being monolingual is a recent phenomenon in our part of the world. South Asia was a multilingual society and manifested in its artistic expression the 'rainbow civilization', as it were. Most, if not all, of the classical and folk poets in this region were polyglots and some of them were equally good in all the languages they chose to write in. Mirza Ghalib and Allama Iqbal are the prime examples from the nineteenth and the twentieth centuries who wrote in both Urdu and Persian. Besides, our mystic poets, from Amir Khusro to Sachal Sarmast, were all multilingual. Those who did not write in more than one language knew other languages spoken and creatively used in the vicinity and in the wider literary ethos of this region, reflections of which can be seen in their work. Bulleh Shah who wrote in Punjabi and Shah Latif Bhittai who wrote in Sindhi are prime examples. In the more recent past, it is also worth mentioning that most of Pakistan's accomplished English-language writers and poets of the twentieth century, Ahmed Ali, Taufiq Rafat, Daud Kamal, and Alamgir Hashmi, to name a few, are all multilingual and fully abreast with the diverse shades of literature in indigenous South Asian languages. Ahmed Ali was in fact a major Urdu-fiction writer as well as one of the pioneers of modern South Asian English fiction with others like Mulk Raj Anand and Attiya Hussain. Since the advent of the twentieth century most major Urdu writers enjoyed a considerable command over English even if they did not use it for creative expression: Allama Iqbal, Quratulain Haider, Faiz Ahmed Faiz, Sardar Jafri, Noon Meem Rashid, Saadat Hasan Manto, Ismat Chughtai, Shamsur Rehman Faruqi, Abdullah Hussein, et al. I remember Professor Sahar Ansari, noted academic, critic, and poet once saying that Iqbal and Haider have raised the bar so high for poets and writers that some erudition and a reasonable command over English is the bare minimum to be able to create a worthwhile contemporary work of literature in Urdu.

Distorting one of my favourite Mark Twain aphorisms, I would say that I too have never let my English schooling disturb my Urdu education. I feel that English to our generation is what Persian was to our literary predecessors. Our parents' generation was in the middle of that transition between Persian and English. Most of them spoke all three languages in addition to a few others. The linguistic affinity between Urdu and English in terms of shared vocabulary may not be the same as it was traditionally between Urdu and Persian, but the language that connects a contemporary Urdu poet or writer with the wider creative and intellectual sensibility of the world is now English. Like our predecessors in Pakistan and North India used Persian for academic and creative expression, it is somewhat natural for Pakistani writers to use English as our other cultural and intellectual language. Nevertheless, one cannot deny the fact that this change in the second language has everything to do with a complete transformation in the dynamics of power, politics, and economy in this region and the world.

English expands your horizons and exposes you to what is being felt, thought, argued, and spoken globally today. How would I have the ability to enjoy classical and contemporary writing in both English and other world languages available in translations into English if I had not known the language? But if you have grown up with classical Urdu poets from Mir Taqi Mir and Nazeer Akbarabadi to Mus'hafi and Mir Anis, and then find yourself surrounded by the works of hundreds of exceptionally talented writers in Urdu and other languages from Pakistan, with a diverse range from Shaikh Ayaz and Ghani Khan to Majid Amjad and Jon Elia, what you cherish is not the language or the desire to seek international audience through that language, but the quality of writing and the ecstasy it fills you with.

Unlike what a number of English-speaking Pakistanis would like to believe, and some of them profess with a hint of arrogance in panels organized at literary festivals or in indulgent op-ed pieces they write on occasion, there is a large volume of interesting and high quality literature being produced in Urdu, Punjabi, Seraiki, Sindhi, Balochi, Pashto, Brahvi, Hindko, Shina, Brushiski, and other languages spoken in Pakistan. In terms of literary worth, a large number of talented writers in these languages will continue to challenge the relatively small number of English language writers. On the other hand, to be able to rub shoulders with the best among their contemporaries internationally, our writers in English need so much more than they offer presently. Therefore, it makes me sceptical when new English writing from Pakistan is seen as archetypal of the literature being produced here and accorded sole representative status. In itself, it does not at all reflect the richness and depth of Pakistani literature. English is just one of the languages in which some of us Pakistanis write—a language spoken, read, understood, and appreciated by very few in the country.

Nevertheless, one must acknowledge that Pakistani English fiction writers in recent years have added a new dimension to our literary experience. They have contributed to linking us with the global writing experience. They have opened new vistas of imagination and expression. But travelling the length and breadth of the country tells me that it may take forever and a day for English to become Pakistan's prime language of creative expression. Whenever I go to a public seminar in a hotel or a conference hall in any Pakistani city, where proceedings are being conducted in English, a large number of people in the audience will remain quiet. Then, when one speaker comes to the dais and switches to Urdu, or another local language, the whole place becomes animated.

In effect, the more people from across classes and secondary towns participate in media and communication, theatre and oratory, the more Urdu and other Pakistani languages will be used. The mushrooming of private television channels, both news and entertainment and FM radio stations have perhaps created challenges for the right usage, pronunciation, correct idiomatic expressions, etc., but the phenomenon has promoted the language and its use like never before. This also means that more democracy and participation, economic growth, and social development will rapidly increase the need for communication between people living in different places, resulting in more Urdu being used. One small example is the commercial nonviability of three English-language news channels in recent years. One was shelved after years of investment and just at the time when it was all set to be launched, the other completely switched from English into Urdu, and the third was shut down after running for a couple of years.

The relationship between Urdu and other Pakistani national languages has also changed over the years, which many older, political workers and cultural rights activists refuse to recognize. While Urdu news, drama, and music channels continue to marginalize English language broadcasting, they grow in tandem with electronic media and publishing in other Pakistani languages. The more that people get involved in political, cultural, and social conversation, more space is created for other Pakistani national languages. Sindhi, Pashto, Seraiki, Hindko, Balochi, and Punjabi channels, as commercial enterprises, may not be making as much money as Urdu channels do, but they are growing and progressing in their own way. A new blend of languages can be witnessed in political talk shows as well as entertainment shows. Some channels actually have bilingual or multilingual programming.

What could not happen in the bureaucracy and judiciary, parliamentary legislation and policy making, educational curriculum and public messaging, is now happening on private radio and television channels where languages are used according to the needs and demands of common citizens. A language whose speakers grossly outnumber its so-called native speakers may start insisting on a standard register, making a variety of stakeholders agree to it, asking people at large to adhere to that standardization, and then emphasizing a uniform accent and a sanitized pronunciation, but this will never be possible— despite my appreciation of these ideals. Therefore, the more Urdu is left on its own, in terms of people using it as they need and as they please, with self-proclaimed custodians of the language stopping their lament about its disgrace and not worrying about its imposition by the state as a national or official language in the true spirit, Urdu will continue to evolve by gaining strength from its sister languages and local dialects within Pakistan, besides borrowing words and idioms from English. It is the lingua franca and the shared language of the people, but not the mother tongue of most. Pitching it against other national languages and mother tongues of the country through half-hearted state patronage over the years has done it no good.

There is another explanation here bordering on a conspiracy theory, I am afraid. When the dominant elite in Pakistan realized that people of all classes and ethnicities have now learnt Urdu and it has become a people's language, they stopped patronizing it. One ruling of the Supreme Court of Pakistan in 2015, invoking an article of the Constitution that asks the state to enforce Urdu as the official language, is not likely to change the course powers-that-be have taken for long. Their children get disempowered and marginalized if Urdu and other Pakistani languages replace English at various levels of public affairs. The struggle will continue for years to come it seems. Hence, I would argue that we take a multilingual path and teach our children two languages or more and teach them all these languages, including English, equally well.

****

However, with all the above arguments and debates happening in the spheres of politics and sociology which provide a contextual backdrop to creative writing, but certainly do not determine its course, when it comes to writing poetry and prose, I will continue to write in the language of my choice that comes to me naturally at that moment of creation: be it Urdu, English, Punjabi, or Persian. Forms, themes, emphases, and treatment may differ from one language to the other, one idea to the other, one instant to the other, and from one place to the other. But for a poet, more important is the poem. The issue of language is paramount in the discourse of politics but becomes incidental in the realm of literature.

Meeraji, the avant-garde poet and one of the trail blazers of modern Urdu verse in the early twentieth century once wrote about himself, stating that ethnically, he is a Kashmiri; in terms of his place of birth, he is Punjabi; and in matters of language, he is an Urdu speaker. He further said that his intellectual and poetic temperament is conditioned as much by the East as by the West. I can fully relate to his statement. I am convinced that art breaks the moulds of all set categories. It subverts conventional and stated understandings of how life and society work, it challenges and overturns established identities, and deconstructs agreed categories of analysis.

Meeraji literally disturbed people with his work because it was so different from what had come before. He did not finish high school but his study of languages and literatures at a tender age was phenomenal. He wrote in Urdu but enjoyed a scholarly command over English, Persian, and Sanskrit. He was prolific and, besides composing poems, he wrote quite a few articles and translated works from Sanskrit, Persian, and European literatures into Urdu. Meeraji experimented with theme, form, and expression within a form. He challenged morally and socially acceptable subjects in Urdu poetry. There is a corpus of erotic poetry and prose in classical Urdu literature but Meeraji treated it with a different technique in a new style. His disdain for sexual conformity made him controversial and he was despised by new and traditional critics alike. While he was badgered for being too open and irresponsible, the paradox is that he was criticized for being too obscure at the same time. Some critics are of the view that this obscurity partly comes from the influence of French symbolists, people like Baudelaire and Mallarme, and attempts to conceal certain abnormalities and perversions to some extents. Meeraji, in the foreword to his collection *Meeraji Ki Nazmein* (Poems of Meeraji), said that the pollution that culture and civilization have collected around sexuality offends him. As a reaction, he saw everything under the sun as the image reflected in the mirror of sexuality, and this image is perfectly natural and it is his ideal. In my opinion, Meeraji has a streak in common with Marquis de Sade but just a streak. Octavio Paz, the arch Mexican poet and essayist of the Spanish language, has critically appreciated Marquis de Sade, the French author who lived in the late eighteenth and the early nineteenth century and spent thirty-two years in prisons and mental asylums. Paz observes that Sade's greatest originality stems from his having thought of eroticism as a total, cosmic reality. But, Sade took it to an extreme by justifying violence as nature and nature as intrinsically evil. Meeraji's eroticism was Indic, where there is a desire to dissolve your being in the womb. But Meeraji was also consumed by his deliriums and disorders.

Meeraji died at the young age of thirty-seven. He was born Sanaullah Dar but adopted his beloved Meera Sen's name as his nom de plume. The legend goes that she was a Bengali girl who lived in Lahore and nothing ever flowered between her and Meeraji, except that the silent suitor changed his own name to his beloved's name, something that hints at Meeraji's character and eccentricities. His poetry is kneaded in his unique personality. The unsavoury reputation earned by Meeraji in his times was not only due to his choice of themes, but equally due to his choice of forms. The modern Urdu poem is indebted to Meeraji (and his contemporary Noon Meem Rashid) for popularizing vers libre, the *azad nazm* in Urdu. Although Tasadduq Hussain Khalid is supposed to have pioneered this genre in Urdu, it was Meeraji and Rashid who painted a fresh canvas of Urdu poetry in bold colours. Rashid took the form to new heights with an ease that comes only to a genius. Neither of them deviated from the traditional prosody and metre simply for the sake of flouting the rules; instead, they created new forms within the tradition to suit their own content and a new sensibility of their times.

I wish to constrain myself to poetry but a mention of the unchallenged master of Urdu fiction, Saadat Hasan Manto, cannot be avoided. Also, because he was born in the same year as Meeraji, 1912, and the two are connected in several ways. Both died very early, Manto died at the age of forty-two, five years after Meeraji. They were both non-conformists who shocked the readers of their times and continue to shock people today. Manto wrote a pen portrait of Meeraji, *Teen Golay*, which appeared in his collection *Ganjey Farishtey*.

The translation of this collection in English was done by Khalid Hasan titled, *Stars from Another Sky*. Manto also wrote a foreword to the translation of Damodar Dasgupta's *Kutni Katha,* by Meeraji, from Sanskrit into Urdu. This translation has recently been reprinted in Lahore under the title of *Nigar Khana*. These two great men, in their own ways, established for us that the liberation of the human body, mind, and soul cannot be selective. It has to be for humanity at large. It has to encompass all aspects of our lives.

In the 1980s, when my generation was growing up in Pakistan and lived under the stifling Right-wing martial rule of General Zia ul-Haq, reading literature gave us solace; and progressive literature gave us hope. There was one man, Saadat Hasan Manto, who invariably made me shiver. His writing caused me sleepless nights. He would take young rebellious students believing in revolutionary politics like myself beyond the compulsions of crass politics and outward social change. There was no one else in Urdu fiction whose work was as nuanced as his and as brave in dealing with the taboos of sexuality. In our early teens, some friends and I would pick up Manto for erotica. But the more I read, the more I understood that this boldness was laced with such subtle emotion and a deep sorrow that no one else could convey. One felt numb and frostbitten: numb after reading *Khol Do* (Open It), a story about a young migrant woman repeatedly raped, and frostbitten after reading *Thanda Gosht* (Cold Meat), the story of a man who turns impotent after finding that the kidnapped woman he is trying to make sexual advances on, is already dead. Through *Toba Tek Singh* (a town in Punjab where the mental asylum of Manto's story is located) and *Tetwal Ka Kutta* (Dog of Tetwal), Manto made me understand the paradox surrounding the Partition of India, with all its surreal undertones at one level and with such directness and simplicity on the other.

Saadat Hasan Manto fills us up with a deep compassion for humanity but tears open the curtains of its dark side without any remorse. In describing his protagonists and their deeds, he employs an ambivalent treatment of good and evil. He neither moralizes nor proselytizes. He neither invokes rancour nor revenge. He inspires you with his insight and wisdom and not by emboldening the contours of a particular political ideology. The oppressors and subjugators are never at peace with themselves, and the humaneness in a cruel man may pinch him hard, from deep inside, at a time when he would least expect it. Similarly, a normal human being without power or pelf has the potential to become a beast in certain circumstances.

Mao Zedong once said that it is suffering alone that transcends the social class of a person. Saadat Hasan Manto was the effortless raconteur of suffering, not just going beyond associating people with their economic prowess, social class, caste, colour, or faith, but also by detaching them from their motivated actions. The worst suffering in Manto's life, for him personally and for the people around him collectively, was the Partition of the South Asian subcontinent in 1947. He kept his critical distance from the event, yet Manto's pen did not hiss but screamed on paper and his fingers did not press but pounded on the keys of his Urdu typewriter as he dissected the religious extremism and communal violence he had witnessed. When you read Manto today, you realize that the predatory times of Partition are not over. In addition to the pain we inflict upon ourselves those inflicted by global powers have also increased with time. Saadat Hasan Manto's writings on 1947 form the basis for establishing a process of truth and reconciliation around this colossal tragedy, the terrible suffering endured by a generation and its never ending aftermath—the aftermath that we saw in Dhaka and continue to see from Srinagar to Ahmedabad in India, and from Peshawar to Karachi in Pakistan.

Partition influenced generations of writers in Pakistan. Whether some saw it as a sheer tragedy, some as deliverance, or some as both, a tragedy and deliverance, all were affected by its enormity. But when it comes to themes and forms, along with the master craftsman Faiz Ahmed Faiz, there are some fascinating poets whose diction, metaphor, similes, and treatment remain rooted in conventional Persian and

Urdu ghazal from Ahmed Faraz, Parveen Shakir, and Ada Jaffery to Shabnam Shakeel, Yasmeen Hameed, and Abbas Tabish. Some of them have written powerful poems besides writing in the traditional ghazal form, but the universal charm and exquisite beauty of the ghazal rhyme and refrain dominate their literary expression. Iftikhar Arif, Aziz Hamid Madni, Khursheed Rizvi, and Jon Elia are unique in their respective styles but have stayed deeply entrenched in the classical tradition. Some of these poets are household names across the subcontinent because without imbibing from the goblets passed on over generations—from Hafiz Shirazi, Omar Khayyam, Mir Taqi Mir, and Mirza Ghalib—to the fascinating poets of our times, no appreciation of modern Urdu poetry, or for that matter any modern poetry in our Pakistani and North Indian languages is possible.

****

Being a poet myself and a student of literature, I find myself closer to the form of nazm, a relatively modern genre, similar if not the same, to the form of poems written in languages other than classical Persian and the languages influenced by classical poetry in Persian. Although, Persian does have a rich culture of long classical nazms, from Nizami Ganjvi's *Haft Paykar* (Seven Forms) to Fariduddin Attar's *Mantiq-ut-Tair* (Conference of the Birds), ghazal is the primary genre. The nazm provides a greater scope for building a narrative in verse than the ghazal (the established classical form with a variety of metre but dependent on refrain with each couplet distinct in meaning from the other). Allama Iqbal was nazm's real harbinger, followed by Josh Malihabadi. But they did not play much with the prosody and form. Some modern twentieth and twenty-first century poets I like for their nazms have written ghazals as well. It is like those who predominantly write ghazals, Iftikhar Arif for instance, have penned some memorable nazms. Arif, whether writing about the martyrdom of the Prophet of Islam's grandson Husain, and his family and faithful in the battleground of Karbala, to composing powerful modern poems like *Kitab Keechar Mein Gir Pari Thi* (The Book Got Dropped in the Slime) has a distinct flavour. Nothing can be defined in binaries, be it people, places, art, genres, etc. One of Arif's nazms that represents the modern, progressive streak in his work, using an old metaphor from Muslim history, is *Abu Dhar Ghifari Ke Liyay Aik Nazm* (A poem for Abu Dhar Ghifari). Ghifari was one of those companions of the Prophet of Islam who championed the rights of the poor and the oppressed, and was not liked by the rich and the powerful. Arif invokes history to explain the present. Arif has employed this technique in many of his important verses.

Speaking of the contemporary nazm, the works of Noon Meem Rashid, Majid Amjad, Fahmida Riaz, Saqi Farooqui, Sarmad Sehbai, and Munir Niazi always had a lot of traction for me. I met Munir Niazi a few times before he passed away in 2006. When I went to see him for the first time, I entered the main gate of his house and found myself in a small garden. I saw him sitting in a room which was lower than the level of the garden outside where I stood. He asked me to jump into the room through a large window, almost like a French window, for he felt too lazy to walk up to the closed door on the other side of the room, which opened into a corridor leading to the main door to the house, which was also closed. When I was jumping in, he said that people have made Mir and Ghalib guard the doors of poetry and, therefore, a new poet has to learn to enter the room through the window. He had set the tone of our first meeting. He said that he loved classical poets but there can be no Mir or Ghalib and not even Faiz and Rashid because we live in different times. The art of poetry is aligned with its time even if it has a long lasting universal message. Living in and glorifying the past too much undermines the equally sensitive and powerful expression of today. Let others bloom as well, it is good for new readers too as they bring a new sensibility and contemporary consciousness. He continued in the same vein. Then he asked me when I came to know him first and if it was through my father or on my own. I told

him how, when young, I once randomly picked up an aesthetically
produced, hard-bound book as a birthday gift for my father. It was
Ali Abbas Jalalpuri's *Rivayat-i-Falsafa* (The Traditions of Philosophy)
where I saw Munir Niazi's name for the first time in print. He was the
publisher of that book. Convinced that I was on his side, he felt a little
charged, got up and went inside to ask for tea. Narcissistic, innocent,
and witty, he was measured, self-possessed, and hugely loveable
whenever I met him. The only poets he ever mentioned to me from
among his contemporaries with admiration and respect were Noon
Meem Rashid, Akhtarul-Iman, and Fahmida Riaz. They can only be
reached if their readers are at a certain higher level of consciousness,
according to him.

I always saw it as a privilege to listen to an exceptional creative
genius unwinding and sharing his feelings and beliefs. The awe, the
range, the uncertainty, and the newness made Munir Niazi the master
of his technique. Once I was asked by an erudite friend, who wants
to categorize and schedule each one of us who writes, whether I see
Munir Niazi as a modernist or a postmodern poet. I told him that
I see him as the 'most modern' poet of our times. And it was not
mere wordplay. I truly believe he possesses a completely different
metaphor and style. Fitting him in a box based on existing categories
of literary analysis is extremely difficult, if not impossible. Even his
poetry that was used in film songs enjoyed mass popularity for its
depth of emotion and fluidity, comparable to none other. Without
using the much-cherished way of *gureiz* (digression with a meaning)
in content or form, he had the ability to take the reader beyond the
narrative through sheer emotion. He had the confidence of writing
a one-line poem for it conveyed what he felt. Then, whether it was a
two-liner or a three-liner, a short poem or a long one, he would not
interfere with his own creative flow by guiding it with the compulsions
of structure, appearance, and detail.

His Punjabi poems share the same sensibility, style, and even
syntactical patterns that mark his Urdu poems. But the richness of

Punjabi idioms are never confronted by his poetic process, which is essentially in Urdu. Something one cannot say about any other poet who writes in both languages. In fact, the poetic process is made more meaningful by introducing words and ideas that naturally came to him from his environs. Among other bilinguals, Faiz harbours a characteristically Persianized diction of Urdu on the one hand and a completely rustic expression in the few Punjabi poems that he wrote. The genius of Iqbal pronounces itself quite differently in both style and treatment when he writes in Persian. Munir Niazi has one corpus of work: Urdu-Punjabi.

Munir Niazi is like an impressionist painter in the realm of our poetry and perhaps the only one of his kind. He would not illustrate his poems with moral lessons by using historic or religious metaphors, even if they were in praise of God or religious figures. With loose brushwork and in a wide array of bright colours, as impressionists would, he painted the landscapes of human life and physical nature, mixing the two effortlessly. The inanimate objects of nature come alive and take charge. Another quality, that is comparable to impressionists, is his flair for using phrases, lines, and similes that are used to swiftly capture the essence of the subject rather than its details, the way impressionists would use short, thick strokes of paint. While there is neither obvious veneration nor disdain for political ideals in Munir Niazi's work, the love of life and nature is uncompromised throughout.

As far as his originality is concerned, Sarmad Sehbai is one of the most original and important artists in Pakistan. With a multi-dimensional and atypical creative talent, he has written poetry, directed plays, and produced theatre. He is also a connoisseur and curator of classical and folk music but here we are concerned with his poetry, particularly his nazm, not ghazals. He may not agree with my view that the best of his ghazals are in the pure classical idiom. His poems are modern and unconventional. His poetry is subversive, eclectic, and unpredictable.

There is an incident from Agha Hashr Kaashmiri's life which was first related to me by my father that reminds me of Sehbai. Agha Hashr, the pioneering dramatist of Urdu, left his home town Banaras to visit all possible *natak* (drama) companies across India in the early twentieth century. He would meet the owners and staffers and humbly tell them about his skill and potential. He would read out passages and dialogues from his plays in a soft voice, if allowed, before getting dismissed. People would not even give him a patient hearing, let alone a chance to write or perform for their companies. One day, he decided to change his style. He barged into the office of the owner of one of the biggest companies in the country. Thespians and business investors surrounded him. Agha Sahib, without any introduction, looked straight into the eyes of the owner and started reading from his work at the top of his voice. After a while, he stopped and asked them all, who by that time were overwhelmed by his presentation, if they knew anyone else in the whole of Hindustan who could write like him? Then, Agha Sahib dictated how the meeting ended. As soon as he uttered these words, mouths of the envious and the malevolent were gagged forever. He got the job.

Sarmad Sehbai has the courage to revolt against the conspiracy of silence hatched against the genuine and the original artist. To borrow terms from Jean Cocteau and apply them to my benefit, I would say that mediocrity is promoted by creating a 'conspiracy of noise' in its favour and genius is suppressed by hatching a 'conspiracy of silence' against it. Although Sehbai is well recognized in all of the fields he dabbles in, he scares the self-proclaimed champions of art and literature in Pakistan. They just would not mention him when due. It must be so unnerving for our entrepreneurs of art and literature, whose skill seldom matches their ambition, that the readership and audience changes after every few years and it is only the brilliant, original, enigmatic, and paradoxical writers that remain. Sehbai also believes in art functioning as a free floating signifier. Utilitarian motives kill it. Art is feared because it is subversive. Art is the beloved.

And the beloved is always unpredictable; they may or may not reveal. Sehbai challenges the overt political character in art, but at the same time, blurs the lines between art and politics and sharpens the contours of human tragedy. For example, by writing a moving poem after the bombing of a Peshawar Church. He also believes that capitalism, through its new corporate apparel, fears art as much as the institutions of the state would. All efforts to reign in art fail to succeed but the powers in place keep struggling. Poetry is wonder and power structures evaporate in the wonderment of poetry.

Sehbai is also one of those who say that their immediate heritage is the Indus Valley and see themselves as men or women of the Indus. He calls himself a Harappan man who is very close to the real poetic tradition of the Indo-Gangetic plain. I see a contradiction here because the Harappa or the Moenjodaro man was someone who came before the modern Indus man or the modern Indo-Gangetic man. I would consider him and those of us who came after him, to be modern men and women with a new sensibility and a brewing urban angst from the aforementioned region. Such women and men can be called neo-natives. According to Sehbai, the richness of classical Urdu poetry is symbolized only in Mir and Ghalib. I agree with him with regards to the canvas of Mir. It is impossible that Mir was unfamiliar with the great poets who preceded him or lived in his times. He was much more indigenous than Ghalib and must have imbibed from Bhagat Kabir, Mirabai, Shah Hussain, and Baba Guru Nanak. That gives his poetry an incomparable strength in the corpus of Urdu verse. Ghalib is the greatest modernist poet, post-modern at places, and someone to be cherished always. It is only Ghalib who could express the inexpressible through playful innovation. Like Shakespeare, who places Hamlet between the medievalism of his father and the renaissance of his own times, Ghalib is amazing for he depicts the existential angst of a man caught between a rising European, and falling Indian civilization. Our likes and dislikes are shaped by our preferences and our circumstances. There can be no competition like sports among writers—not even contemporaries, let alone among those who are a century or half-a-century apart from each other.

Sarmad Sehbai dismisses Iqbal for being terribly oratorical without bringing his own self into what he said. In my opinion, Allama Iqbal is the most powerful poet of the twentieth century with such a broad range that only few can embrace. One of my favourite contemporary Indian fiction writers is Arvind Adiga, whose riveting narrative in his novel, *The White Tiger*, exposes the grinding poverty and worthlessness of human life in rural India, the limited opportunity for the underclass in a metropolitan city, and finally the resolution that the only option left for the downtrodden to emancipate is to cheat, kill, and commit crimes. Adiga is highly imaginative in in his prose and when the main character takes his poor nephew out sightseeing, he mentions Iqbal, the great poet, and says that he was so right. The moment you recognize what is beautiful in this world, you stop being a slave. This line comes from one of Iqbal's couplets. Adiga further states that the Naxals and their guns shipped from China can go to hell. If every poor boy in India learns how to paint, that would be the end of the rich in India.

Baal-i-Jibreel (The Wing of Gabriel) is an outstanding collection of poetry. Iqbal's work in Persian, like *Javednama* (Song of Eternity), is in a class of its own. Iqbal lived under colonial rule and faced the colonial gaze from up close. Sarmad Sehbai and I continue to face it one-hundred years after him. For us, it is from a distance, but for Iqbal it was piercingly close.

Nevertheless, like Sehbai, Fahmida Riaz remains unconvinced regarding my argument about Iqbal. Even after translating Maulana Jalaluddin Rumi's work into Urdu, she finds herself unable to negotiate with the work of Iqbal, Rumi's disciple in our part of the world. In my view, Fahmida Riaz is a major poet, the most unique in her diction and metaphor, like Munir Niazi, who continues to challenge and subvert the dominant and the obvious in our writing. She and Kishwar Naheed are not just two arch feminist poets in

Urdu, but they have collaborated and worked closely with, inspired, and provoked women younger than them, writing in all languages in Pakistan. Attiya Dawood, Rukhsana Preet, Hasina Gul, and Amar Sindhu are some of these women who deserve a mention here. They write in Sindhi and Pashto. Fahmida has a definite contribution to the reshaping of the landscape of Urdu poetry. In recent years, she has taken to prose and penned some extraordinary short stories and non-fiction.

Fahmida has a knack for inviting trouble. She has gone through a difficult personal and political life and lived in exile in India during General Zia ul-Haq's martial rule. But when she visited India after the demolition of Babri Masjid by religious zealots in 1992, the subsequent Hindu-Muslim riots, and the massive communal violence, she courageously read a brilliant poem titled *Tum bilkul hum jaisay nikley* (You turned out to be exactly like us!). She is a free soul, believes in pro-people democratic politics, has relentlessly struggled for human rights and women's emancipation all her life, suffered greatly for being radical and uncompromising, and continues to suffer. She is a vocal supporter of peace and friendship in South Asia but when she wrote the poem and first read it out in a mushaira in India, she was threatened and yelled at by a section of the audience, hence, forced to leave the premises. But the ability to differentiate between what could be an isolated incident and what is a universal reality is crucial. The crookedness of certain individuals, petty issues that mar a certain kind of people, and an all-pervasive wretchedness we find in organizations pursuing political gains may cause short-lived bursts of anger in poets and artists like Riaz. But such behaviour or events fail to dilute the unrequited love they have for humanity.

****

Fahmida Riaz's humanism brings to mind another great personality of Maki Kureshi, who I admire but did not have an opportunity to meet. Yet, some of her poems that I read while young, haunt me to this day. She was older than Fahmida and lived in Karachi for most of her life. Kureshi was of Iranian-Zoroastrian descent and was married to Abu Kureishi, the elder brother of Pakistan's famous cricket commentator and journalist, Omar Kureshi. She is undoubtedly one of the best English-language poets from our part of the world and along with Taufiq Rafat, Ghulam Fariduddin Riaz, and Daud Kamal, led the way for other important poets like Alamgir Hashmi, Adrian Hussein, Salman Tarik Kureshi, and Waqas Khwaja. There is a definite quality to each poem she composed. Every once in a while I pick up *Wordfall*, an anthology of three poets published in 1975 by the Oxford University Press, including Kureshi, Taufiq Rafat, and Kaleem Omar. The selection from her works was also published in 1997 by the same publisher. Besides bringing immense pleasure and a sense of literary accomplishment, her work also goads my social and political consciousness in a distinct way. As events impact nations, words impact individuals. Kureshi's language, imagery, and introspective awareness of the world she belonged to contributed to shaping the inner feelings and outward approach of many of her readers including myself. I insisted on using her work, against the will of my supervisor, when writing about a social science subject for my post-graduate degree. This was at the expense of losing marks for quoting from poetry. But, like love, poetry is magic. The nineteenth century French poet and politician, Alphonse de Lamartine, once said, 'Sad is his lot who once at least in his life has not been a poet.' But sadness has many dimensions and both, as a poet or as a reader of poetry makes one feel sad.

Maki Kureshi's poem 'Kittens' had a strange effect on me the moment I read it. The effect has become an imprint. It once again confirmed the limitations of our discourse and made me feel contrite about these geopolitical debates, notions of imperialist and anti-imperialist agendas, and sensational journalism—print and electronic alike. In 'Kittens', Kureshi writes about her cat being dismayed, slinking away after delivering too many kittens. There were so many that they could not all be adopted by kind friends either. She then writes about her relatives advising her to take them to the bazaar and letting them go, each to her destiny to live off pickings. But the poet is wary because, being so small, they could easily be stepped upon, kicked by shoes, battered by heels, or eaten up by gaunt street dogs. They may also starve to death. Then she remembers that the European method is to drown them in warm water. She writes that warm water is advised to lessen the shock and the kittens are so small, it only takes a minute. You hold them down and turn your head away. She describes what will happen in the water, the callous details. Then she reassures herself and the reader that since they are born blind, they will never know who did this to them. The water will recompose itself. Kureshi asks herself which method she should choose snagged by two cultures? Poetry has an enormous impact on the reader. Love is a demon and so is poetry.

Taufiq Rafat was also born in the same year as Maki Kureshi, 1927. He died three years after Kureshi, in 1998. It was hammered into my head from a tender age, by my father, that John Donne is the poet to be read if I am at all interested in English poetry. If I am writing in Pakistan, two people I must know who have heralded original English-language poetry in South Asia are Nissim Ezekiel, the Jewish-Indian poet from Mumbai, and Taufiq Rafat, the poet based in Lahore. After reading them both I realize that some indoctrination in such matters is good for young people. I wanted to meet Rafat and hoped that he would write a preface for one of my collections of poems in English. The arch Urdu novelist, Qurratul Ain Hyder's brief but affectionate mention of Rafat in one of her books was also in my memory.

I met Jalees Hazir, Rafat's son in Karachi at his cousin and my childhood friend Faisal Butt's place, who himself is a poet. I was told by Hazir that Rafat has been a recluse for a long time and does not meet people. If he does meet someone and listens to their poetry he does not comment. He has not written for years either. I still wished to meet him, even if he would not say or write anything. An invitation was extended to me and I made a plan to fly to Lahore.

It was the summer of 1998. In Karachi, the usual numb dampness was suspended in the air. My younger brother rushed me through the busy Shahrah-i-Faisal in our mother's antique Toyota Corolla. I vividly remember that a crisp, freshly folded copy of the daily newspaper, *Dawn,* was presented to me by the airhostess just a few minutes after I had settled down into my seat. The back page of the newspaper had a two-column news story announcing the death of Taufiq Rafat. Imagine you are all set to travel to meet a person you revere and suddenly find that the person died just a day before. I was lost and left totally dazed by the circumstance, but the travel to Lahore could not be relinquished at that stage. I was sitting in the aircraft. I chose to spend the day in Lahore with my friends and relatives and simply lolled about. I went shopping into those clever, large, overbearing, and unwieldy bookshops on The Mall. It was simply impossible to muster enough strength to attend Rafat's funeral.

Rafat's poetry lightens your heart by crying out loud for all the dear ones you have lost and then smile at the saplings noiselessly cracking the earth beneath you. British writer and poet Adrian Mitchell said that most people ignore most poetry because most poetry ignores most people. This is exactly where Rafat comes to poetry's rescue. His poetry relates to people. It embodies a diverse range of their pains and pleasures. His poems are earthy, rustic, rooted in the wryness of being on the one hand, and its ecstasy on the other. There is an exquisite paradox in all his writing. It is about the soil, the human beings, raindrops, seasons, toads, owls, pigeons, kicked dogs, mango trees, grass, loneliness, family, aunts, uncles, cousins, fasting, Eid, and the much beloved younger brother.

There are two streams, as it were, in Pakistani English poetry. One, is the kind of poetry that could have been written anywhere in the world and has an archetypal English idiom. The other stream is poetry written in English whose universality is rooted in local experience and idiom. The poetry you cannot write without having experienced and internalized a life lived on the land we tread, and having read Bulleh

Shah, Baba Farid, Khawaja Fareed, Shah Latif, Kabeer, Mirabai, and Mir Taqi Mir. Rafat has given Pakistani English a voice of its own and is one of those who led the way in naturalizing English as one of the several Pakistani languages. His *Poems for a Younger Brother* (sixteen in all), the series of twelve poems under the title *1978, After Many Hot Days, A Kicked Dog, Pigeons,* and *Dew* call to be read again and again.

****

People are enamoured by poetry but poetry, as a form of art, is also at the receiving end by some serious opinion makers in Pakistan. It is not just the conservative thinkers who reject poets, essentially because they are considered non-conformists, but some rational prose writers and academics express the same opinion about the futility of poetry. One of our leading progressive historians, celebrated for popularizing a pro-people interpretation of history—different from subaltern history though—Dr Mubarak Ali, dismisses poetry regularly and has published articles on the subject. His unmatched erudition and historic insight have enriched us for decades. But when he claims that our love for poetry as a people is responsible for our current dismal state of social and intellectual affairs in Pakistan, it is seriously questionable. Coming from him, such a linear and superficial line of argument is mind boggling. A book of literary writing, that he himself helped translate and edit with Razi Abedi some years ago is called *Achhoot Logon Ka Adab* (Literature of the Untouchables), which also contains exquisite translations of Dalit poetry. It has run into multiple editions.

The treatise of dismissing poetry begins with the classical claim that historians see progress in human civilizations as a journey from simplicity to complexity. It may be fine up to this point. But when it is said that in the age of simplicity, poetry was the main vehicle of expression and when civilizations grew it was replaced by prose, this is an over simplification. Categorizing poetry as only limited to emotions is problematic. It is said that since poetry is rhythmic and easier to memorize, it is recited to each other and in public gatherings. Prose replaces poetry in analysing and critiquing the social, political, and economic issues when a civilization has developed. During the development of Greek thought and civilization, it is argued that Homer's 'Iliad' and 'Odyssey' and Hesiod's 'Theogony' were replaced by the intellectual effort of natural philosophers and their subsequent writings in prose. By this argument, the epic poems of the Indian civilization like the 'Mahabharata' and versified 'Vedas' are relegated to a secondary position compared to the 'Upanishads' and 'Puranas', later written in prose.

Such rationalists maintain that poets were relegated to an unimportant position after the Industrial Revolution and the rise of capitalism. Their position was bolstered by people like Rousseau, Voltaire, Hume, Smith, Ricardo, and Malthus. These thinkers could respond to the challenges posed by the modern world in the making. Later, people like Herder, Kant, and Hegel steered the change process in the German mind. The comparison made between philosophers and poets, in such simple terms, is reflective of a purely instrumentalist understanding of history. The grand narrative is so predominant, that these critics seem to forget that we are human beings first and that all social, political, and economic phenomena affect us. There is something called complexity of emotions and depth of imagination which also comes with changing times and changing circumstances; individuals transform when society transforms, or vice versa. Where does that individual or collective search for meaning find its expression? Besides, there are fundamental questions of being and existence which may well have been resolved by some out of an enforced convenience, but such issues continue to stare us in the face as there has been no final resolution.

If poets were relegated to an unimportant position in modern Europe, as a result of developments in other disciplines, why is Shakespeare still so relevant, not only for the people in England but also to the rest of the world? Why do Germans celebrate and remember Goethe with such fervour? What about the Romantics—Byron, Shelley, Keats? Why are T. S. Eliot, Sylvia Plath, and Ted Hughes quoted from and referred to in any substantive conversation across many countries? Simply put, the arguments made in the first place by the critics of poetry, the comparison they make between poets writing poetry, and thinkers writing prose is wrong, and the conviction that one is superior to the other is also wrong. They have their own separate domains of thought and expression. Both are equally important to understand nature, humanity, society, and our collective perpetual quest for a more meaningful existence. It would be strange, indeed, if we created a contrast between creative writing and sociology and then argued over which should be preferred or which should be shunned for the other.

These ideas ignore the ever expanding horizons of creative non-fiction and the role of fiction in dominating the realm of prose in today's world. It seems that the changes introduced in the forms, styles, and genres of poetry in most languages of the world over the last century are also completely overlooked. There is blank verse, free verse, prose poetry, and entirely non-rhythmic compositions. In older, more tested forms as well, there is a blossoming of new ideas, expression of feelings, and presentation of thought processes, etc.

Coming to Pakistan, critics of poetry squarely blame poetry for its inability to analyse social and political issues rationally. But is that really the role of poetry? About our noted resistance poet Habib Jalib's poem on the new Constitution promulgated by the military dictator, General Ayub Khan, in 1962, it is said that when Habib Jalib recited his poetry in public gatherings, people became emotionally charged and were inspired with revolutionary ideas. But as soon as the recitation was over, no lasting impression was left on the minds of the audience. His poem became very popular but failed to highlight the contents of the Constitution and its harmful impact on society. On the other hand, it is argued that when a political scientist writes about the Constitution and rejects it, she/he first analyses the provisions and acts of the Constitution, which are anti-people, but protects the privileges of the ruling classes. Such scientific analysis creates a political awareness among the people in order to fight against the Constitution. However, poetry falls short of that and merely raises slogans, providing no rational tools for struggle. I challenge this understanding.

In fact, the only lasting impression we have on our minds from the resistance offered to the Constitution imposed by the first military dictator of Pakistan is Habib Jalib's poem *Dastoor* (Constitution). Who in this world compares a poet rejecting the anti-people and anti-democratic nature of a Constitution with a social scientist or a lawyer examining the Constitution clause by clause? Both are important and both are necessary. Artists and pieces of art contribute to expanding the horizons, sharpening the sensitivities, and enriching the consciousness of people. People and societies do not change overnight. Who enriches us more than Ghalib? Interestingly, Faiz's poem *Hum Dekhein Ge* (We Shall See), is sung as an anthem by political workers in Pakistan and India. Even some Naxalites recite it in their gatherings in remote parts of India.

Moreover, there are modern Urdu poets like Noon Meem Rashid, Majid Amjad, Fahmida Riaz, and Sarmad Sehbai who introduce you to another consciousness and a contemporary expression of feelings. Our languages, other than Urdu, also have a long list of such poets. More than ever, in Pakistan, we need poets, creative writers, painters, and thespians to make us a more tolerant, humane, sensitive, and civilized society. I fully agree with the assertion that we need social scientists, thinkers, and philosophers—not just poets. We need to contribute to serious prose, undertake rational analysis and examine our circumstances, create awareness, and bring about social change. However, that does not mean that all who write poetry should switch to writing philosophical pieces. Poets do not stop others from reading, thinking, and writing prose—creative or analytical. Many poets write prose themselves.

This, in fact, is the Hegelian view against poetry that is professed and propagated. In the words of Terry Eagleton, the Hegelian view is: art as a mode of cognition must now yield the pride of place to philosophy and truth must vanquish the sensory. But Hegel saw art as an unconscious affair. It was problematic then and it is problematic now. In the middle of the twentieth century, a similar argument was made in different terms by Jean Paul Sartre. In one of his essays, he dismisses poetry from the list of literary genres worth considering because poets are concerned with words purely for their own sake and not as a means of communication. This idea is fashionable with some other thinkers, perhaps also in the tradition of Plato. But Plato alluded to poetry as much as he criticized it. Poets have the liberty to treat words affectionately or contemptuously, snatch away a longstanding meaning from them, or give them a new meaning. They reinvent communication and then communicate with the reader or listener much more subtly and deeply. I do not believe in any hierarchy among different genres of art and literature. But poetry has a certain ecstatic charm and a lasting impact, which at times is latent and at other times obvious.

I do see a lot of merit in his argument when Sartre says that although literature is one thing and morality another, there is a moral imperative at the basis of each aesthetic one. Morality here for Sartre and for many of us, by the way, is not about conformity, dogmatism, religiosity, and tradition. It is about freedom and equality. Poetry and morality—when morality means coded behaviour and grim structures—are totally at odds. If voluntary, which in case of creative writing and its readership they are, the acts of writing and reading are both acts of exercising liberty and 'free will' and, therefore, acts of love, courage, defiance, and resolution.

****

But yes, artists and creative writers, including poets, are different in their mental make-up from other scholars and intellectuals: the way they feel, the way they observe, and the way they experience life and objects around them are all different. People are familiar with works in English, from Dr Kay Redfield Jamison to Michael Schmidt, the lives of mostly European and American writers are analysed, psychoanalysed, their inner selves discussed and debated, mood changes and suicidal tendencies studied, and the relationship of manic-depressive illness with the artistic temperament is explored. Also, any such book written anywhere that offers a psychoanalytic study of literature and literati cannot perhaps be complete without a commentary on Shakespeare and his protagonists. Something truly pioneering that Shamim Ahmed has done for us in Pakistan in recent years is to help us understand the psyche, spirit, inner soul, and essence of a few leading Urdu poets and writers. In his work, *Torment and Creativity*, Ahmed's embrace is large. He has taken a methodical approach, employing his study of psychology to appreciate some literary geniuses.

From Freud and Adler as theorists in psychology to Shakespeare and Tolstoy as creative geniuses, Shamim Ahmed's embrace is both large and gripping. He has expanded his study to include Saadat Hasan Manto, Sahir Ludhianvi, Ismat Chughtai, the Bronte Sisters, P. B. Shelley, T. S. Eliot, John Keats, Tennessee Williams, Faiz Ahmed Faiz, Allama Iqbal, Noon Meem Rashid, Shafiq-ur-Rehman, Ibne Insha, Edgar Allan Poe, and Yagana Changezi. Ahmed's objective inquiry and subjective celebration makes the book unique. His objectivity prevents the book from becoming undemanding and light, while his subjectivity makes it absorbing and readable. The author has treated the people he writes about with a lot of compassion. This compassion, unlike the contemptuousness we see prevalent, comes from the depth and the expanse of someone's knowledge. Besides other psychological conditions, neurosis, and bipolar disorders, Ahmed has described the 'cognition of the universality of pain' as a big impetus for creativity and art. That is where pro-people politics comes into full play in the realm of creative writing. In our own case, that is how we can explain the aesthete in Faiz Ahmed Faiz also becoming an ardent trade unionist and the aesthete in Kishwar Naheed struggling all her life for justice and women's rights.

Undoubtedly, the value of any work of art, poem, or painting is determined by its aesthetic appeal. However I find the creative process most gratifying and the work produced highly valuable when the chaos outside dissolves into the chaos within; the exclusivity between 'art for art' and 'art for life' is withdrawn. Indian-Urdu poet, Akhtarul Iman's *Daasna Station Ka Musafir* (The Passenger for Daasna Station) is about the role memory plays in defining the subtle pain, the containment of hurt, and the bitter-sweet aftertaste of love. Not only does it blur the delicate line between teenage infatuation and profound love, it emboldens the separation from and longing for each other by the lovers, brought about by the migration of people after Partition.

One who has experienced persecution, oppression, and victimisation (woman or a man), feels differently from those who are sensitized but have not experienced it. The anti-fascist Italian poet and writer, Cesare Pavese, once said that a lonely man who has been in prison, goes back to prison every time he eats a piece of bread. Another person can empathize but cannot feel the same way. But, writers are different: especially those who create emotion in readers and their imagination makes them experience what a victim has actually felt.

When there is a clear undertone of subverting power and privilege, woven into a definite optimism for the wretched and the condemned, and the two are knitted together by a thread of romantic imagination, aesthetic appeal does not get compromised. This 'knit' is the intricate work of a tailor and not the stitching of a cobbler, whether the tone of expression is subtle or obvious. I have to confess that this understanding is rooted in my own experiences of life, longing, suffering, and creativity. This is the view of a Pakistani writer with a specific background and history with existential and ideological underpinnings. For instance, when going through its worst cycle of violence, Karachi produced its most powerful creative responses which did not compromise the aesthetic demands of a work of art. They came from Asif Farrukhi in the form of his two short story collections and Zeeshan Sahil in a series of poems.

Art has the power to subvert and the power to heal, sometimes separately and sometimes collectively. From Bulleh Shah celebrating the character of a prostitute in his Punjabi poetry, composed in the eighteenth century—how she is able to detach herself from her physical being to the woman of easy virtue—to Guy de Maupassant's remarkable story in French in the nineteenth century 'Boule de Suif', poetry and literature overturned the conformed social order. Besides, the wounds that even a collective understanding of history may not heal, literary treatment has the power to heal. Even if the perpetrators and victims alike established and accepted that Hindus, Sikhs, and Muslims were killed in hundreds of thousands and all communities were equally responsible for unleashing terror on each other in 1947, the wounds inflicted on each other will not heal. Wounds can only be healed by the poetry of Amrita Preetam and the fiction of Saadat Hasan Manto, who have converted 'Hindu suffering' into 'human suffering' and 'Muslim tragedy' into 'human tragedy'.

Creativity never ceases to hatch conspiracies against despair. From the cold valley of Hunza in the North to the warm swamps of Badin in the South, we laugh and we cry, we sing and we dance, we paint portraits and we draw cartoons. We tell stories and we compose poems. When celebrated author, Dr Ashiq Hussain Batalvi, met arch scholar, Dr Syed Noman-ul-Haq, sometime before Batalvi passed away, he told Dr Haq, 'Noman, sanoo te sheir ne bacha leya' which virtually meant that poetry is our only saviour. Long ago, George Eliot said that art is the nearest thing to life.

Notes

Preface

Ghalib, Mirza Asadullah Khan. *Divan-i-Ghalib* (Urdu), Fazleesons, 1997.

Eagleton, Terry. *The Liberal Supremacists*, Column in *The Guardian*, London, 25 April 2009.

Aslan, Reza. *No God but God: The Origins, Evolution and Future of Islam*, Random House, 2005.

Worthing, John. *Report on Richard Dawkins' interview on Bill Maher's HBO show*, *Sunday Express*, London, 30 November 2015.

Harris, Sam. *The End of Faith—Religion, Terror and the Future of Reason*, W.W. Norton, 2004.

Grossman, David. *Writing in the Dark*, Picador, 2009.

Barnes, Julian. *Flaubert's Parrot*, Jonathan Cape, 1984.

Blood

Donne, John. The line is from the poem *Twickenham Garden*, published in *The Collected Poems of John Donne*, London: Wordsworth Editions, 1994.

Manto, Saadat Hasan. *Tetwal Ka Kutta* is a short story included in the collection titled, *Yazeed* (Urdu), Maktaba-i-Jadeed, 1951.

Narayan, R. K. *A Storyteller's World*, Penguin India, 1989.

Mahabharata, a Sanskrit epic considered holy in Hindu faith and the longest poem ever written.

Ramayana, a Sanskrit epic poem ascribed to Valmiki, a Hindu sage and poet.

Burke, S.M. *Jinnah: Speeches and Statements 1947–48*, Oxford University Press, 2000.

Khan, Mohammed Ayub. *Friends, Not Masters*, Oxford University Press, 1967.

Bazaz, Prem Nath. *History of Struggle for Freedom in Kashmir*, Kashmir Publishing Company, 1954.

Khan, Nur. Report with the heading *Nur Khan reminisces '65 war* in the daily *Dawn*, Karachi, 6 September 2005.

Sweat

Hikmet, Nazim. The line is from the poem *On Living*, (translated from Turkish by Randy Blasing and Mutlu Konuk), published in *Poems of Nazim Hikmet*, Persea Books, 1994.

Bashir, Ahmed. *Jo Milay Thay Raastey Mein* (Urdu), Al-Faisal Publishers, 2011. *Dil Bhatkey Gaa* (Urdu); Sang-i-Meel, 2012.

Niazi, Zamir. *Press in Chains*, Karachi Press Club, 1986); *Press Under Siege*, Karachi Press Club, 1992; *The Web of Censorship*, Oxford University Press, 1994; *Hikayat-i-KhoonChakaan* (Urdu), Fazleesons, 1997.

Faridoon, Mahmood. *Murder of Bhutto*, Patriot Publishers, 1988.

Ishaq, Major Mohammed. *Hasan Nasir Ki Shahadat* (Urdu), Ishaq Academy, 2008. (Urdu text from the interview of Hasan Nasir given to Mohammad Ali Malabari quoted in Ishaq's book is translated into English by Dr Kamran Asdar Ali and included in his book, *Surkh Salam*, Oxford University Press, 2015).

Khan, Dr Aftab Ahmad. *Bayad-i-Sohbat-i-Nazuk Khayalaan*, Dost Publications, 2005.

Hussain, Sadiq. *Afsanay* (Urdu), Book Home, 2012.

Ali, Agha Shahid. Lines from the poem, *Lenox Hill* in the collection titled, *Rooms Are Never Finished*, W. W. Norton, 2002.

Tears

Rilke, Rainer Maria. The line is from the poem *At the Brink of Night* (translated from the German by John Burnham), available on www.poemhunter.com.

Mazari, Sherbaz Khan. *A Journey to Disillusionment*, Oxford University Press, 1999.

Eagleton, Terry. *Culture and the Death of God*, Yale University Press, 2014.

Mar, Khet. *Night Bird and Other Stories*, Sampsonia Way Publications, 2015.

Ink

Angelou, Maya. The line is from the poem *Caged Bird*, published in *The Complete Collected Poems of Maya Angelou*, Random House, 1994.

Mir, Mir Taqi. *Kulliyat-i-Mir*, Sang-i-Meel, 2013.

Shah, Bulleh. *Kalam Bulleh Shah*, Uloom-o-Irfan, 2016.

Bhittai, Shah Abdul Latif. *Kamil Darvesh*, Fiction House, 2015.

Fareed, Khwaja. *Divan Khwaja Fareed*, Al-Faisal, 2011.

Farid, Baba. *Baba Farid-ud-din Masood Ganjshakar*, Sang-i-Meel, 2007.

Meeraji. *Kulliyat-i-Meeraji* (Urdu), ed. Dr Jamil Jalibi, Urdu Markaz, 1988.

Paz, Octavio. *An Erotic Beyond: Sade*, translated from the Spanish by Eliot Weinberger, Houghton Mifflin Harcourt, 1998.

Manto, Saadat Hasan. *Ganjay Farishtay* (Urdu), Maktaba-i-Jadeed, 1953; *Thanda Gosht* (Urdu), Maktaba-i-Nau, 1950; *Namrud Ki Khudai* (Urdu), Maktaba-i-Jadeed, 1952; *Siyah Hashiyay* (Urdu), Maktaba-i-Jadeed, 1952; *Phande* (Urdu), Maktaba-i-Jadeed, 1954.

Noon Meem Rashid. *Khwaab Le Lo, Khwaab* (Urdu), Ed. Tauseef Tabassum, National Book Foundation, 2012.

Amjad, Majid. *Kulliyat-i-Majid Amjad*, ed. Khawaja Mohammed Zakariya, Mavara, 1989.

Iman, Akhtarul. *Kulliyat-i-Akhtarul Iman*, Aaj, 2000.

Ganjvi, Nizami. *The Haft Paykar*, translated from the Persian by Julie Scott Meisami, Oxford University Press, 1995.

Attar, Fariduddin. *The Conference of the Birds*, translated from the Persian by Afkham Darbandi, Penguin Classics, Re-issue edition 1984.

Arif, Iftikhar. *Written in the Season of Fear*, translations from the Urdu by multiple translators, Oxford University Press, 2003.

Niazi, Munir. *Kulliyat-i-Munir* (Urdu), Mavra, 2007.

Sehbai, Sarmad. *Pal Bhar Ka Bahisht* (Urdu), Alhamra, 2008.

Iqbal, Mohammed. *Kulliyat-i-Iqbal*, Iqbal Academy Pakistan, 1990; *Javid Nama*, translated from the Persian by A. J. Arberry, George Allen and Unwin Ltd, 1966.

Adiga, Arvind. *The White Tiger*, Free Press, 2008.

Riaz, Fahmida. *Sab Lal-o-Guhar* (Urdu), Sang-i-Meel, 2011.

Naheed, Kishwar. *Dasht-i-Qais Mein Laila* (Urdu), Sang-i-Meel, 2001.

Rafat, Taufiq. Kureshi, Maki. Omar, Kaleem. *Wordfall*, Oxford University Press, 1975.

Shamsie, Muneeza, Ed. *A Dragonfly in the Sun*, Oxford University Press, 1997.

Kureshi, Maki. *The Far Thing*, Oxford University Press, 1997.

Rafat, Taufiq. *A Selection*, Oxford University Press, 1997; *Half Moon*, Taufiq Rafat Foundation, 2009.

Ali, Dr Mubarak. *Past, Present: When Matters Get Verse*, Column in *Dawn Sunday Magazine*, 3 August 2014.

Jalib, Habib. *Kulliyat-i-Jalib* (Urdu), Mavara, 2007.

Sartre, Jean Paul. *What is Literature?* Translated from the French by Bernard Frechtman, Washington Square Press, 1966.

Jameson, Kay Redfield. *Touched with Fire*, Free Press, 1993.

Schmidt, Michael. *Lives of the Poets*, Phoenix, 1998.

Ahmed, Shamim. *Torment and Creativity*, Ushba, 2014.

Maupassant, Henri René Albert Guy de. *The Cocotte (Boule de suif) and Three Other Stories*, Franklin Watts Ltd, 1971.

Eliot, George. *Selected Essays, Poems and Other Writings*, Penguin Classics, 1990.

Acknowledgements

FIRSTLY, I WOULD LIKE TO EXPRESS MY GRATITUDE TO MUHAMMAD Ismail Khan for asking me to write these essays, and to him and Faisal Buzdar for providing me support when most needed. I am indebted to Sabahat Iqbal Ashraf and Natasa Durovicova for their critical editorial advice. During the course of writing this book, the grave personal losses I underwent were the deaths of Mushir Anwar and Mahjabeen Mushir—my beloved Uncle Mushir and Auntie Malka. I will always miss the sudden and tragic end to that rich cultural dialogue in their living room which remained uninterrupted for decades. I am certain that their only son, Khayyam Mushir, will cherish and promote his illustrious intellectual heritage. Around the same time as the Anwars, Aslam Azhar, a distinguished exponent of art and letters, passed away. He was a constant source of inspiration. The three of them in their own individual ways influenced my thinking, some of which is reflected in this book.

I am thankful to Ashfaq Saleem Mirza and Zaffar Abbas for helping me organize my initial thoughts. While revising the drafts, it is important to acknowledge the useful insights I gained from Dr Kamran Asdar Ali, Safiya Aftab, Salman Asif, Taimoor Shahid, Bilal Naqeeb, Sara Azfar, Ali Akbar Natiq, Dr Amir Jafri, and Mushtaq Bilal.

Besides new thoughts and subjects, events and people, a few themes discussed in these essays have appeared in brief, piecemeal, or raw form in my articles published in Pakistan, India, the UK, and the US in the dailies *Dawn, The News International,* and *The Hindu*; weekly *The Friday Times*; monthly *Herald*; and, in *The Annual of Urdu Studies, University of Wisconsin*. I am grateful to the editorial teams of these publications for giving me the opportunity to express my views.

I started work on these essays earlier but what afforded me time and space to finish the first draft was my stay as Writer-in-Residence at the International Writing Program (IWP), University of Iowa, US, in the autumn of 2015. I am grateful to the wonderful staff and volunteers of IWP for making my time memorable in Iowa City. Also, the team at 'City of Asylum', a cultural and literary organization based in Pittsburgh, US, deserves a special mention for the love they extended towards me and appreciation of my work. However, all this would not have been possible in the first place if Shabana, my better half, had not taken it upon herself to single-handedly run the household and mind our little rascals when I was away.

Finally, a big thank you to the welcoming team of Coffee Planet, F-11 Markaz, Islamabad. They would pump me up with tankards of Long Black whenever I got tired of my study and used their lounge as the alternative workspace.

Index